Insights & Illuminations

"Whether you are new to Spirituality or have been exploring for some time, you will want to read, (and re-read) Gwen Peterson's Trilogy of the Soul...I found the material to be insightful, educational, and experiential with a generous dose of humor. When I first approached the book, I thought, I can knock this out in an hour or two... (ha, ha, ha, as Gwen's Non-Physical friends would say) There is a depth and complexity to the narrative that really makes you pause and reflect on the material, and questions. In addition to the "story", Gwen offers real "hands-on" practical tools to awaken, and/or deepen your relationship to Spirit, Soul, and Self."

Denise Flood
Spiritual Recording Artist

"Kept my interest. I found it entertaining and a relatable way of conveying some of life's important lessons for happiness and spiritual wellbeing."

Shelby C. Peterson
Seeker

INSIGHTS & ILLUMINATIONS

3 COMPLETE BOOKS
To Unleash Your Playful Soul and
Transform Your Life

GWEN PETERSON
FIRST EDITION

INSIGHTS & ILLUMINATIONS

3 Complete Books To Unleash Your Playful Soul and
Transform Your Life

This publication is designed to provide accurate and authoritative information in regard
to the subject matter covered. It is sold with the understanding that neither the author
nor the publisher is engaged in rendering legal or other professional services. While the
publisher and author have used their best efforts in preparing this book, the purpose
of this book is to educate and give suggestions. The authors and publisher shall have
neither liability nor responsibility to any person or entity with respect to any loss or
damage caused or alleged to have been caused directly or indirectly by the information
contained in this book.

Printed in the United States of America

First Edition

ISBN: 979-8-218-10056-8 – paperback
ISBN: 979-8-218-10057-5 - eBook
Library of Congress Control Number: 2022922290

Cover Design by:
Melissa Clampitt
Interior Design by:
Chris Treccani

It's A Game!

———

Puzzle Pieces

———

Your Soul Connection

DEDICATION

Dad, thanks for guiding me in Spirit all these years. Lots of love to the special people in my life; Shelby, Misty, Linda, and Becky. Thanks for the over two hundred combined years of love you have given me. All that love is what keeps me going. A shoutout to Spirit in all its forms, I love you.

CONTENTS

INTRODUCTION

———

Have you ever read a book or watched a movie with so many moving parts you felt you needed to read or watch it again and again? Each time taking away a new nugget of information or insight? This will be such a book for you. It may not seem like it, but this trilogy has a lot of content and will speak to you at different levels and at different times of your life. You will **feel** drawn to read it and reread it. My suggestion is to read the first book, *It's a Game*, and sit with what you have read. Maybe reread it before beginning *Puzzle Pieces*.

We have Earth Angels in our lives long before we know what they are. They say or do something that changes us on the inside. One of my professors at Michigan State University was one. I was a freshman frantically trying to pass his class. I needed his help on writing my thesis. He said he would help me although he didn't normally tutor his students. If I was sincere in wanting his help, he would. He started by saying that he would share something with me. Something that I needed to remember in my life.

> Everything in life has three levels.

Using a book as an example, he explained how the words on the page were the first level. The second level would be the meaning behind the words. The third level was the higher meaning behind it all.

His words struck me, but I wasn't sure exactly why he wanted me to know this. The words would come back to me from time to time and I would smile at his wisdom. Now as I sit writing these books, I am again struck by his wisdom.

These three books are laid out in those three levels. The first book, *It's a Game*, the first level of knowing. Using my professor's analogy, we will work with what you are able to see, touch and feel on this third-dimensional planet. The second book, *Puzzle Pieces,* represents the second level of knowing. It is the *feeling* the words carry, the vibration of Spirit. The third book, *Your Soul Connection*, is the third level of knowing. Your relationship with your Soul. Your relationship with Spirit. Your connection to Divine knowledge and the All-Knowing.

It isn't necessary for you to understand all three levels. Just know that everything in life has three levels of knowing and life can be about learning to navigate them. Together we will explore some ways of looking at our lives from those levels.

BOOK 1:

It's a Game!

———

A startling event leads to
a lifetime of discovery

PART ONE

Let's Get Acquainted

——

This book will **not** be an outline of my spiritual journey; that would be somewhat boring. Instead, I hope to give you a different perspective of your life. A perspective on life that I have come to know as Truth. My journey has drastically changed the foundation of what and who I am today. It has occurred in layers. *It's a Game* will be the first layer. I think it makes a little more sense when sharing these topics, to paint it with a little real person correlation and let you hold it up for comparison to your own life experience. How best to gauge life? Not so much from the judgey kind of gauging, but rather a detached kind of thing.

I will try to share with you the highlights of my journey to date and how I came to be sitting here typing away. It will not be a complete telling of my life experience. My journey has been, and continues to be, a crazy path of twists and turns and some of it won't be relevant right now. It is important for you to know that this is **my** journey. Yours, whether you are just discovering it or are much further along, **will** be different.

> Your story will be different.

You have probably come to this book because of the many questions you have in your head. Why is life like this? Who am I? Why do I *feel* stuck? As we move through this book, the questions will not stop, but I hope to show how you can find your answers. Let me ask you a question or two. What about your life are you ready to keep? What beliefs are you going to hold onto for a little while longer? Maybe you aren't ready to answer these just yet. You may find that you need to put this book away for a time to allow yourself to begin processing the words and the *feelings*. Then, when some time goes by, you may *feel* a nudge and wonder, "What became of that book filled with crazy notions?" You will seek it out because you will find that you are ready for more. Or you may resonate with it so thoroughly now, you *feel* pushed to keep reading and embrace your journey from this new perspective. You may feel as if a part of you wants you to know more, with that your journey has started, my friend.

As this book was coming together, it was suggested to lay down a little foundation for the reader. What will this book be about and what can be expected? Heavy questions for a book that has been channeled. For those new to the term channeling and spirituality in general, this book is a lot of both. It is my journey and Spirit's message. I will apologize now if my book makes you shake your head and say, "What?" I did a lot of that myself over the years. It is part and parcel of taking concepts and experiences and finding words to articulate them. I Trust that on a Soul level you will understand because that is why you are reading this book.

Much of this book is channeled from a number of Archangels and Ascended Masters, Spirits from the higher dimensions I have come to know. All wanting to share knowledge with those who are nudged to read this book and play The Game in a more profound way.

Let me share a little more about channeling as I have come to know it. You will find that channelers have a slightly different take on what exactly channeling is, but most would agree that there are two different ways to channel, trance and conscious. Most would agree that channelers and mediums are different in regard to whom they are channeling.

- **Trance channelers** such as Edgar Cayce, Jane Roberts, or more recently, Esther Hicks, completely withdraw their conscious mind and allow Spirit to flow and speak through them. Trance channelers are completely unaware of their surroundings and what is being communicated through them.

- **Conscious channelers** such as yours truly are folks who are, for the most part, aware of their surroundings and share what they are "hearing" from Spirit. They must quiet their mind to listen; many conscious channelers do their listening in a meditative state. The thing to keep in mind with conscious channelers is they are filtering the messages they receive through their belief systems and life experiences. These messages are interpreted by the channeler.

Suffice it to say, I am a conscious channel. That means that I do not withdraw my conscious mind. I do have to quiet my mind as best I can to interpret Spirit's vibrational message. I do not hear their messages with my ears but have learned to interpret their vibrational messages I receive. Some conscious channelers turn the flow of Spirit on and off. I do not. I have trained myself to hold open that channel for information. It is like having an antenna that I didn't have before. If the Archangels and Ascended Masters need to share something, I will hear their vibrational message.

Keeping that antenna tuned to their frequency makes it easy for me to check in on any guidance I may need.

Through my personal practice I have done quite a bit of Soul work that allows me to dialogue with my Soul more fully for guidance, as well. Holding the energy of both of these vibrations takes practice and creates an integrated personality of sorts. What you are reading here is not trance channeled material nor my third-dimensional mind. It is that blending of Soul and Spirit coming through. Sometimes my mind will jump in and ask questions and judge what I am receiving and *feeling*. Those moments will be shown in thought bubbles to allow you to see how this all flows. Chances are those thoughts will be similar to the ones you are holding.

Take note while reading: Whenever I use words that are capitalized mid-sentence, it is referencing the Spiritual aspect of the word or the Higher-level meanings, they are not typos. Self, You, Soul, Trust, Love, Friends, for example, are the higher aspects of those words. It allows you to begin playing with the nuances of the multidimensional game you find yourself in.

More about me. I was raised Catholic and went through most of the Sacraments. Don't get me wrong, organized religion has its place. I mention organized religion because what happened to me that day in the car on my way to work wasn't anything we covered in church or catechism. That day would be the turning point for me. It set me on a lifelong endeavor to learn what spirituality is. Many who are committed to an organized religion are quick to point out to those peering into spirituality, how they believe in God and Jesus, heaven and hell. As if a person who begins a spiritual quest leaves all that behind somehow. I have discovered that spirituality is nothing more than a person's personal journey into who and what their beliefs are around God and Jesus, heaven and hell, among a whole host of other concepts that come up like death and rebirth, Love and Trust. Some explore their spirituality while involved in their organized religion and others leave organized religion only to stumble onto their spirituality. I am of the latter. I assure you, having been raised Catholic, channeling Angels and *feeling* nudges from my Soul were not the lessons taught in our weekly catechism class. Instead, it looked and felt more like a good dose of guilt. Guilt about everything. A *feeling* I wanted to be free of. My quest to *feel* better and understand myself led to even more questions that gnawed at me. Where would I find the answers to the unexplained experiences in my life? The church wasn't prepared to offer answers and I soon found I wasn't prepared for the answers that would come from my asking.

Story time. Maybe this will let you see why I was asking questions.

My mom asked me one morning if I wanted to skip school. It seemed a distant relative had passed and mom wanted to know if I would want to go to the funeral with her and my grandma and grandpa. I would have normally jumped at missing a day of high school, but for some reason it didn't *feel* right. Not a guilty *feeling* but an 'uh-oh this *feels* like trouble' *feeling*. I tried to brush it away, but I heard a voice in my head that said, "No." So, I didn't go to the funeral.

Later that day after school, I got strange phone calls from family members wanting to talk to my mom. Strange she wasn't home yet.

"Wasn't she with you at the funeral?? What's up?"

"Nothing, have her call when she gets in."

Finally, my mom calls. She would be home late as she was at the hospital with Grandma and Grandpa. The car they were in was hit in the funeral procession; they were not hurt too seriously but needed to be kept a little while longer for more tests.

It was things like this that made me stop and say, "Hmm, what would have happened if I was in that car?" It was questions like this that made me ponder the bigger questions: why did I *feel* that 'uh-oh' *feeling*, and who said, "No"? It was those very instances I came to know later as channeling. The nudge was from my Soul and the words were from my Angels/Spirit.

Answers weren't easy to come by back then. The few spiritual books that existed were located in the back of the store next to the bathrooms filed under "Wicca." Not front and center and labeled Self-Help. The books at that time seemed to stir up more questions than they answered. There were lots of books on channeling. What is that? People talking to Spirit or crossed-over Loved ones? Only folks in the Bible talk to Angels and God, right? Right?? So confusing.

Let's Begin

Begin where? Isn't that the question we ask about spirituality? Then some spiritual smartass tells you, "Begin where you are." Like that is helpful in some way. It will be years until its meaning can be fully understood, much less the enormity of its meaning. Spirituality is like that. Big questions with small answers that turn out to be huge answers to small questions.

Yet, that is all that you have. Begin where you are. You will want to take an inventory of what that looks like for you in this moment. It may be a little scary depending on when this question hits you. Addiction, bad romance, there are a lot of things we can get ourselves caught up in. You may very well be reading this book because life isn't exactly what you had hoped for.

Stop for a moment and think about where you are in your life right now and make a few notes. Things to consider: employment, abundance, and relationships. What is happening in your life? It is important to give yourself this moment to reflect.

_____

_____

_____

_____

_____

Then there are the questions.

Why did this happen and why should I do anything at all? What is the purpose? Does it really matter? Remember I mentioned the questions will just keep coming. If you like, note them here. You will have your chance to look for these answers later.

I have questions. What about this book? Why am I writing it and for whom? I don't remember signing up to do any of this and I hope speaking engagements aren't the next thing to follow. Do I hear faint whispers that this is not the only book? I think I can hear laughing out there somewhere too. I guess I should start laughing too and you, my friend, will laugh later when you get Spirit's joke in all this.

_____

_____

_____

_____

_____

Welcome To Gwen's Mind

Hello, Gwen here. Welcome and have a seat somewhere. You are going to take a ride. A chance to get to know who I am so far. You may have already seen that these writings will be full of innuendos, what have yous, and whatnots. Partly or mostly because there is no better way to share with you this journey, which will culminate in a book guided by those you will come to know and written by a person who has found herself caught up in a very strange life experience far from where she thought she would be.

Many of my closest friends and family have no clue of the trials, tribulations, levels of awareness, and not-of-this-world happenings that I have encountered. Until now, I have only shared it with a handful of friends in my spiritual circle. How does someone begin to share such information with those they love and hope not to lose because of our Soul's choices? Better I put it down on paper and let everyone make their choice of whether to see this side of me exposed or not.

The nudges for this book have been coming for a while now. When I would stop to think about it, I couldn't even start to imagine where it would go or even begin. Pieces have been coming to me and I have written them down on scraps of paper and in journals. Almost all of them have been lost or thrown away over the years. In some distant way I knew that when the time came, I would sit down and tap into my connection with my Non-Physical Friends. The Friends I have come to Know and Trust in such a deep way. Their guidance would flow and make sense to those they are meant for.

Conscious channeling at its best. This has been going on for a number of years, decades, I guess. They have introduced themselves over the years and more come through as the years move on. I am referring to the Archangels, Ascended Masters, and a few others that may get introduced as we go on or not. For the most part, 'They' are who I have come to call the Mentors, Lords of Light, or simply Friends or Spirit. The name is irrelevant; it is just a placeholder for the big explanation of who and what. This group comes through me and steers me

> It has been an interesting ride so far and I have gotten better at being the driver and host.

through so much of my work and day-to-day experiences. They have been so important in the founding of the Spiritual Communities Network, Insights and Illuminations, and my life in general over the past quarter century. Hmmm, I am getting a nudge here reminding me of those moments when I was really young and I was hearing and *feeling* their presence. Funny how we dismiss things and then later look back and go "Oh yeah!" I guess I didn't have the understanding in those younger years and just filed them away.

So far so good, my Friends. I am liking this flow of our story together. Now the conundrum. Where do I want to go from here? My mind wants to take over and decide how this story goes. It wants the words to make sense and follow some rhyme or reason. Perhaps following a specific storyline that has been laid out in a thousand different ways by those who would say how a book should look and sound. But for the moment, I think I will stop. Tomorrow will be another day to pick this up and let Spirit lead. The editing will come later.

Here I sit doing what *feels* like the hundredth time of reading and rereading and I *feel* a nudge. How did we leave out the whole Soul thing? I won't delve too deeply into a conversation about the Soul. Definitely a discussion for another time. Suffice it to say, my

Soul has a very active part in all of this as well. The nudges. Those would be my Soul. Nudge, Nudge, Nudge. Nudge. Nudge.

It is my hope you will see the flow of The Game even as I write this book, listening to Spirit and following the nudges of my Soul as I put this book together. Even though channeling can be a lot of listening, it is also a *game* of paying attention to your life experiences.

For instance, talking with a friend completely independent of my book, they mention a book they heard of called—Are you ready for this? —*The Game of Life and How to Play It* by Florence Scovel Shinn. IKR! You can't make this up. I hear my mind say, "We don't need to continue *this* book as it has already been done." My Non-Physical Friends are quick to point out that it is time for this information to be made relevant again.

I did a little research, you know. The two books will be similar, yet different, in their depiction of The Game. It may sound strange, but it is comforting to know Florence Scovel Shinn's book is out there. If you are reading this book, it all worked out well and I hope you will enjoy the strange way this is strung together. You see, knowledge of Ms. Shinn's book comes after years of beginning to write this book. I am maybe 2/3 of the way through. It is a confirmation for me. A Universal wink if you will that I am on track and need to continue to get this done at this time. I Love Universal winks. They help me sort out my mind and its concerns. The comforting *feeling* is my Soul agreeing with the process. Thank you, Friends, for sending the moral support.

Here is another beautiful slice of serendipity. Ms. Shinn wrote the book at a time when Alice Bailey was busy channeling Djwal Khul a.k.a. The Tibetan a.k.a. DK. Take note as Djwal Khul is part of my spiritual journey too. Just a little FYI and maybe a short story at another time.

Suggestion as we move forward: If you can, don't let your mind try to jump ahead on topics. It may say to you that it knows this stuff already, but I assure you, my Non-Physical Friends involved in the creation of this book are turning a few things on their head and you will want to be cognizant of their subtleties. It may be less confusing that way. Okay, proceed, my friend.

That Fate Full Day

Often nuggets will come through during my morning meditation practice and I just hop onto the computer, open this file and I skip around and add what is coming through. Today is my writing group day. As I sit looking at the somewhat blank page, I can *feel* the nudge to share the story that is at the root of this book and it causes me a great deal of angst in sharing. Ready, set, go!!

It was sometime during the early 1990s when I was trying to figure out how to get out of the funk, I was in. I seemed so depressed. Why? I had a good paying job—not that I Loved it, but the money was there. I was married. Things seemed good there; we were building our new home and we were excited about that. We were vacationing in beautiful places and I had great friends to hang out with. How is it possible to not be happy? But I wasn't. Not in the deepest part of me. I had for a few years been listening to Jack Boland at Church of Today.[1] He was televised and I had bought a number of his taped talks. An amazing man and teacher. I loved listening to him. He could lift that heavy *feeling*. He made me want to understand what he was saying on a deeper level. I wanted to experience life the way he described it.

Heck, I had a 45-minute drive every day to and from work, so why not listen to my buddy and find my happy spot. This particular morning, as Jack was talking, I hadn't realized I had kind of slipped into a meditative state. (I hadn't begun a meditation practice yet and wouldn't understand this moment for a long time.) From that deep space, I remember just kind of silently shouting at God, "What the hell is this all about anyway? Tell me!! I am tired of *feeling* like this."

Suddenly I was jolted back to reality by a bunch of people yelling, "It's a game!" I quickly realized I had zoned out and was now flying 90mph into a sharp turn on the freeway. I laughed and thought, "Okay, I got my answer and now I am going to die."

A Game?

I braked heavily, got the car under control, and reflected on what the heck happened. The voices had been so clear and loud like the owners of the voices were sitting in the car with me. As I thought about it more, I noticed that I recognized the voices. Grandma, Grandpa, Harland, Dad, and others. Wait. These people are all dead. Dad died when I was five and I should have no idea what he would sound like. Yet I knew. I knew in my heart of hearts it was him. (As I reread this for editing, I can *feel* his hug and his love fills my heart. Where is my box of tissues?)

What the heck was that!!!

What game? Even though I was asking the question, I was *feeling* the answer. I could *feel* the Truth in the words. I could *feel* some of the heaviness of my funk lifting.

As I continued my drive to work, my body felt really strange. I could *feel* the fabric of my clothes, the actual threads as they crisscrossed to form the fabric. And I could *feel* the pores of the leather that covered my steering wheel. I also began to notice that I was aware of another presence within me staring out of my eyes and taking things in. I could sense a *feeling* that I had never felt before. Unconditional Love. **The absence of judgment.** It was the most amazing *feeling* and one that I knew was not of this world. It radiated from whatever was now sharing my body with me. I observed its observing and I just sat in that *feeling*, soaking it in and wishing that I, too, could find that unconditional loving essence of that being within myself. Was that even possible?

When I got to the office, I called my sister and told her what was happening to me. Her suggestion was to not tell anyone about this. I would be locked up. It would be another ten years until I rendezvoused with the people and resources to answer the bazillion questions I now had. And another ten years to sort out this Game thing.

> Now I find myself sitting here writing what I have come to know and not quite sure what that will look like to you, telling a story that until now I have shared with very few people. But to share with everyone in a book how I continued to travel down that rabbit hole and found myself thrown deeper and deeper into the limitless Love that is Spirit—well, that may be a whole different story. Some, I am sure, will feel I have blown a fuse somewhere. Where will this book go now? I think I will step away and let this revelation on paper sit.

The D&D Metaphor

Funny what you find when you open your eyes to things. I have pondered in meditation what this book could possibly look or sound like? All the bits and pieces didn't seem to make sense to me, and what about 'The Game'? I knew somehow the book was going to be about The Game we are playing here in the third dimension and considered the idea that maybe this would incorporate a game. Maybe spelling out the goal of The Game, rules, directions? I just couldn't see it though. I couldn't *feel* it because I was too caught up in my mind. I kept thinking about the many games I have played and which of those would best resemble my mission here. Once I quieted my mind in meditation, though, and allowed myself to listen, I felt nudged to check out *Dungeons & Dragons*. I had never played *Dungeons & Dragons* but basically grew up with the knowledge that it was a game that tended to draw in fanatics for it; cosplayers and LARPers (i.e.: live action role-playing where players immerse themselves in their characters and act out their choices, like an unscripted play).

> I went to MSU and there were always stories of D&D games being played in the steam tunnels and the urban tales of kids losing themselves in the game and disappearing, never to be heard from again. How would this game be similar to what I am working on?

I was *feeling* called to go to the bookstore in search of this game.

I asked my daughter about the game of D&D and she wasn't

> Does the bookstore carry games?

sure it would be helpful as D&D isn't a board game. D&D is made up of books on "how to play the game" as it is a role-playing game, or RPG. LOL Do you see the fun Spirit is having already with this?

So off to the bookstore to see what my next puzzle piece looks like. May I say that it did not let me down. I picked up the *D&D Player's Handbook*. As my daughter said, there were a few books on how to play the game and some game pieces for purchase, but I stuck with the *Player's Handbook*, which appeared to be a very detailed description of the 'game.'

As I flipped the pages, I just laughed. Twenty-five years and here was The Game spelled out in *Dungeons & Dragons*. I guess if I hadn't lived through these years the way I did, the book I was holding wouldn't be resonating with me in the way that it was. It wasn't a book I would be reading in its entirety, yet I could see there was a lot for me to appreciate. I was mesmerized by the synchronicity of things and could *feel* that I had uncovered a big piece of the puzzle and on a much higher level. I purchased the book. My daughter was happy with my decision and eager to get her hands on it when I was done with my research.

> I will let you know now that this book you are holding will NOT have that kind of content.

Let me start by saying how the layout of the *D&D Player's Handbook* is amazing. The work that has been poured into it and the depth of content is, well, amazing, all 300 plus pages.

Like the Shinn book, there are aspects these books will share, but I can *feel* this going in a different direction.

I looked at it from how it was laid out.

> Is this how I should fashion the layout of my book?

I could *feel* it was something more than this. Maybe if I read it, I will see why Spirit directed me to this book. I started with the preface and … wow. The first page I read of the *Player's Handbook* had the most far-reaching depth for me. I could *feel* the words and

> Could I be that inspiring?

Loved the message Mike Mearls shares with the beginners about how to play the game.

I realized I didn't need to read much further. How would I incorporate what I was *feeling* from these words into my book?

A Cliché

Let me share with you about this past month as I have been haunted by the words of Mike Mearls. So much so that I am using the quote here and hope that I don't break some copyright or plagiarism rules. I truly have to wonder if the folks who created this role-playing game, or RPG, were aware or are aware of the overlap between D&D and the real-life game we play here on planet Earth? I would like to think they do. Okay, here is the part that really haunted me this past month. Mike Mearls writes,

> "The first characters and adventures you create will probably be a collection of clichés. That's true of everyone, from the greatest Dungeon Masters in history on down. Accept this reality and move on to create the second character or adventure, which will be better, and then the third, which will be better still. Repeat that over the course of time, and soon you'll be able to create anything, from a character's background story to an epic world of fantasy adventure. Once you have that skill, it's yours forever."[2]

I hope you can *feel* the depth to these words as it is your Soul's story. The role your Soul plays over and over again in many lifetimes. I suspect I will have reason to revisit this analogy in the future. For now, let's play with cliché.

The word just kept going around and around in my head. It touched my Soul. Mr. Mearls' use of the word cliché. It kept popping up in the work I do. Often, I *feel* called to step out of my comfort zone and do something I know nothing about. One such thing is writing social media posts. I want to create engaging posts on social media. I really want to be inspiring with my words. At first, the words are those that have been used a million times and are, OK, boring, or cliché. But as I keep working at it, the words are starting to flow easier, and with time they will have more depth and meaning. When I hear the word cliché echo back at me when I begin a new project, I *feel* relieved that I don't have to be a master out of the gate.

Fast forward. I am still writing this book (lol) and am sitting in my writing group today. I didn't *feel* any great information to write and opted for a little editing. Read, reread, look for some type of flow so as not to lose you. Having read the above paragraphs, written a couple of years ago, I am struck by these words again. Do I mention my sixtieth birthday is tomorrow? When I was young, sixty seemed so old. Today COVID-19 continues on, my divorce is final, my mother has transitioned, and I have cut cords with toxic relationships, to name a few of the many things that have happened so far this year. I have had a lot of new beginnings and every time I began to doubt myself or kick myself for not being perfect, the word cliché would pop in and I would take a deep breath and allow myself to move through it without the need to be perfect. In this moment, I am the freest I have ever been on so many levels of my being. I *feel* very young and *feel* I am reinventing myself. Who do I want to be when I grow up? I am excited to be creating a new life story. Such a far cry from the girl in the car.

Spirit is sharing with me that this book will be a lot like the cliché. It will be very general on a number of topics. Somewhat third dimensional in its telling. It is meant to give you the lay of the land and confidence to begin playing The Game. I suspect this gentle reminder is also a heads-up to me that there will be other books to come that will address the higher levels of work I do. It will be interesting to see how this work will tie in with the classes I have been teaching. I can *feel* a gentle unfolding of something much bigger than I am able to fully grasp in this moment. Can you *feel* it too?

A Reminder

A quick reminder as you get ready to read and digest the information presented in Part Two. My interpretation of The Game has come through years of my own spiritual practice and I continue to discover new Truths. What I share is what I have learned and continue to practice in my day-to-day living. Am I perfect at The Game? No, there are times I *feel* like a cliché. Other times I see miraculous things happen in my life and I question how these things are possible. There are things I have been taught to believe are impossible. I want to believe they are possible. I have found questions like: who am I, what is this all about, why is this happening, are nudges of the Soul for me to go deeper into learning who I am.

My meditation and journaling practice set the stage for so much of my understanding about spirituality. Spirit has nudged me toward materials to read that were confirmations for what I was learning from Spirit. My personal experiences taught me to Trust my Soul and Spirit. Learning to allow myself to *feel* the loving presence of my Soul has been an incredible journey that continues to make itself manifest in my life.

Spirituality is not a one-and-done thing. It is ever growing and evolving. As you read Part Two, take time to see how you *feel*. What things resonate with you and which ones don't. Find a quiet place to sit with your reactions. Some of what I share may rub against old belief systems. Is it time to let those go? Only you can know that answer. It is my hope to empower you in finding **your** answers. Don't let anyone tell you. you can't. If something I say resonates in your heart, play with it. If it doesn't, move on. The beauty of The Game is you and your Soul learning to play together.

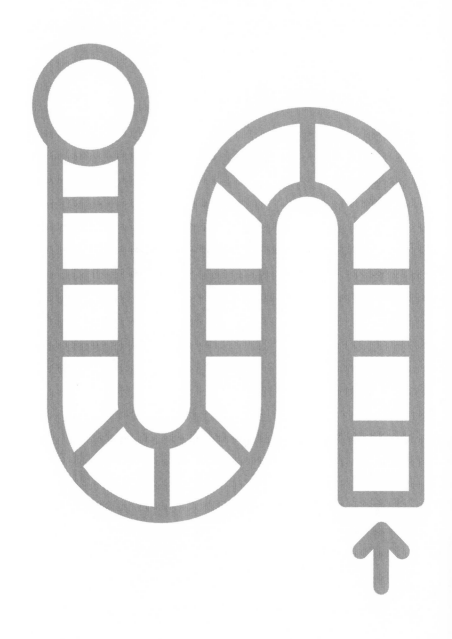

Part Two

Let's Begin to Setup The Game

———

As with any game, you eagerly open it up. You pull out the instructions and read them to better understand how the game will be played: how many players can play, how to set up the game board, and so on. Sometimes you find the instructions on the inside of the lid. The games I have purchased recently have instruction booklets. Consider this your instruction booklet to playing this Game we call life.

Ready?

Game Pieces

Each of these are capable of becoming very lengthy discussions in and of themselves. We will discuss these in greater detail later. For now, let's get the lay of the land with a simple explanation of each. Some of these you have heard me use and may have an understanding of already.

 Avatar - You and Other Physical Players

 Soul - The Eternal You.

The Mind - The thing you think with all day.

 Ascended Masters - Souls that have mastered The Game.

 Angels - Non-Physical higher-dimensional beings.

 Guides - Many of the indigenous peoples relate to Spirit Guides versus Ascended Masters and Angels. I often call all of these higher beings guides.

 Third Dimension - The tangible universe we live in.

 God - All-That-Is, White Light, Unconditional Peace, Love, and Joy. There are many names, we will use God in this book.

Setting Up the Board

This part you really don't need to worry about. There are many game boards being played on many dimensions but for this particular Game we will focus on third-dimensional planet Earth. It has already been set up for you to begin playing the day you were born.

What is the big deal about the third dimension? A lot of people talk about it and reference it. Some may have a vague knowledge of what it really is. It helps to have a strong understanding of what the third dimension is and is not.

In the third dimension:
- Vibrational energy moves really slow.
- We have the ability to touch and taste.
- 'Things' exist.

- Time and space exist.
- We use a thing called the mind to follow cause and effect.
- 'Things' appear to be solid.
- The appearance of death happens.
- We create limitations like age, time, money, and education.
- Thoughts/beliefs become things.
- We believe in darkness.

All the above give us a linear game board to play in. The above items only exist in the third dimension. The higher dimensions have faster moving energy, causing things to lose their solidness  and time, space, bodies, minds and such, for the most part, do not exist. That is what makes this the perfect place for Spirit and our Souls to play. It is so completely different from any other dimension. Maybe think of it in terms of the straw that breaks the camel's back. The camel goes along and then it is the one straw that changes everything. Monkeys go along like monkeys do and then the one-hundredth one changes everything. That is the third dimension. The straw. The one-hundredth monkey. The place of time and space. Instead of everything happening all at once in a primordial soup of energy

> Is this where I need to interject one of my many personal experiences that ground some of these ideas into my mind in such a way that I couldn't argue with it unless I wanted to call myself crazy? I can feel the nudge to continue. It is funny because I hadn't thought of that moment in a really long time.

constantly morphing in all ways at all times, Vibrational energy pretty much comes to what would appear to be a grinding halt or suspended animation. Welcome to your game board.

A really long time ago, I was having one of my deeper meditations where I was communing with Spirit. Letting my mind observe the higher dimensions with my Soul. This was an experience unlike any I had had before. It is when I met Mother Mary. I know, I know it sounds crazy. I can *feel* my ego alarm going off as I type this memory for you. In fact, that was what brought me out of my meditation. My mind had become active and was like, "What was that?" When I opened my eyes and began to anchor back into my body, I felt really different, almost like the car ride that changed my life. As I got up to move around, I felt like I was moving through water. I am not a diver, but I have sat on the bottom of a pool. That is the *feeling* I was having. The air was so tangible and heavy that I thought I could float if I wanted to. In that moment, I realized what 3D really was. Very slow, dense moving energy. To this day, I ask myself, could I have floated if my mind would have let me?

Keep the idea that 3D is just slow-moving energy in mind going forward with this book.

Players of The Game

The Avatar

You, my friend, are the avatar. It is the physical beingness that you call you. The body that you can touch and feel and see in the mirror.

Let's stop for a moment and visit with your avatar. Of course, this isn't an exhaustive list but it will get you started in thinking about you, the avatar. Here are a few suggestions.

Begin with your physical appearance:
- The easiest and most obvious is the race you chose.
- What about your nationality?
- Your sex and your relationship with it.
- Move on to hair. Consider the color and type or lack thereof.
- Eye color.
- Body size and shape.

Doing good so far. Time to go a little deeper with:
- Religious upbringing and affiliation.
- Family or lack of family is another determining factor for your Game piece.

Let's go deeper still and add into the mix your life experience to date:
- Education level.
- Income level.
- Marital status.
- Health.

Stop now and begin to describe your avatar. This may be good fodder for a journaling session as you can go pretty deep into this, if you choose. Find more paper if you need it.

_____

_____

_____

_____

_____

_____

The Soul

Heads up on this one. If you are coming to this book not knowing much about spirituality at this point, give me a moment to paint a little background of what I have come to know about the Soul. It may get deep pretty quick, so pace yourself and let yourself process how you *feel* about what I am sharing. It is not necessary for you to embrace all of this in one sitting. See what *feels* good to you and put the stuff that doesn't on the back burner. Maybe make a note to yourself to revisit it.

Consider the fact that you are sitting here with this book in hand because of your Soul. Your Soul is the eternal part of you, the part that never seems to age. It is as much a part of you as the avatar you described earlier. Your relationship with your Soul comes through as emotions. As we become aware of our Soul, we are able to build a dialogue of sorts with it. The Game allows us to observe ourselves, our mind, and our thoughts and live life more from the Soul's perspective. A perspective that allows us to see the various games going on and understand more fully that The Game of Life is not happening to us, but rather we are actively playing The Game and influencing it.

Okay, we have a Soul but what **is** the Soul? The Soul **is** Vibrational energy **and** an extension of God. Stepped down energy because we are in the 3D world of slow-moving energy, but it is still made up of Unconditional Love, Peace, and Joy energy that is God. We tend to *feel* our Soul in our heart center. For instance, whenever you experience something that makes your heart sing, *feel* full of Love, or moves you to tears, that is you resonating with your Soul. You are in what is called alignment with your Soul. Other times it can come through as a hollow *feeling*. Like there is something missing. Maybe a sense that something needs to be done. This is your Soul attempting to get your attention because you are focusing on something not in alignment with who you are and brings less than Peace, Love, and Joy. This awareness is the beginning of building a relationship with your Soul.

A little bit more about the Soul before we move on. Your Soul resides in dimensions that are not linear. It is in an eternal now moment. A now moment for your mind would be like not thinking about the past or future. Instead, being present in what is happening right here, right now, taking in all the senses at once without any of the limitations of the 3D. Don't worry if your mind isn't ready to go there just yet. That is where the Soul comes into play because from its vantage point, it is in the eternal now moment and has access to Divine Wisdom. It already knows your past, future, and highest good and chose this very life experience.

God

Let me give a little background on the role God plays in The Game, or rather what God isn't. In The Game, God is not vengeful or a man sitting on a throne somewhere casting judgment on all. He is not tallying points for condemnation on judgment day.

Instead, begin to play with the idea of an infinite unconditional loving presence; Vibrational energy really. But if it helps to think of it as a "him" or other anthropomorphic being, that is fine as long as it is infinite Unconditional Love, Peace, and Joy. God is in and through all things. There isn't anything that you can point to that isn't God's energy in some form. Maybe you are *feeling* a fuzzy *feeling* in your heart center?? That is, you resonating with your Soul's Truth and feeling God's Love.

What is the relationship between your Soul and God? I asked this same question of Spirit one day and it was explained to me like this. Consider your body as a representation of God. Now as your attention travels to the fingertips, you are traveling through the slower moving dimensions of Spirit. Ultimately, the very tip of your finger is your Soul in the third dimension. As the finger and fingertips have their experiences, so does God. It is through the Soul that God is able to experience itself. Over seven billion ways and that is just here on this planet. Did I give you too much at once? Revisit with this later. Let's move on.

The Mind

Ah, the mind. The thing you think with all day long and won't let you sleep at night. It is exclusively found here in The Game and attempts to keep control of the avatar. It is what anchors your Soul to this game board.

What makes each avatar unique and brings lots of depth to The Game is the mind. It has been studied and dissected. It has been tested and electrocuted. It has been given lots of names and attributes, like ego, consciousness, subconscious, and so on. Many books have been written and therefore, I will not go into those details here.

Let's keep it light and simple for the essence of The Game. Without the mind, your avatar can't get things done. It is the part of us that identifies with "who we are." The mind creates habits, thoughts, rationalizes, holds beliefs, and interacts (all those things you sometimes wish it wouldn't). It is quite able to operate on its own and is a very useful tool in 3D.

There are a few things you want to keep in mind though about your mind. *Pardon the pun. lol*

- **It should NOT be allowed to run on autopilot,** or say, unattended. We don't really begin to understand this rule until we become self-aware. That awareness thing I talked about earlier. The moment when your Soul begins to get your mind's attention and causes it to say something like, "Hey, what or who was that?"

  As you grow and get to know these two halves of the 3D whole that is you, you begin to see how much the mind is a lot like a three-year-old child. Meditation and journaling practices really accentuate this and is the reason why so many people give up. Who really wants to willingly sit for any length of time with a whining three-year-old? Just look at the parents of a three-year-old. It takes a lot of moxie to hold the course. Getting your mind under control is one of the biggest aspects of The Game because you really don't want an unattended three-year-old running your life.

- **It only knows the past.** Your mind has been fed a diet of fear over the years and has become very fearful as a result. It is ready to regurgitate past failures, losses, and injuries. The mind also knows that its days are numbered. This just adds to the fear component of The Game.

- **It cannot see into the future** and therefore—you guessed it—it can be very afraid of the future.

- **Any changes in your life experience can scare your mind** and begin a thread of fearful thoughts that end with, "and then we will die." Without even thinking about it, we usually cut the mind off when it begins this downward spiral. But "stuffing" these fearful thoughts away doesn't stop them, either consciously or unconsciously. Think minimizing your open pages on your phone or computer. They're still running.

Ah, the unconscious mind rears its head. Round and round your mind will go, waiting for the most inappropriate moment to explode like a stink bomb or hand grenade. You know, like a three-year-old having a temper tantrum. You've seen it. Someone didn't get a napkin in their to-go order and the explosion begins. Anyone standing near takes a step back. All those stuffed down emotions exploding everywhere.

- **The mind is happiest** when it has a job to do and is reassured that all is well.
- **GIGO-Garbage in, garbage out**. Whatever the mind has been fed, it will regurgitate. Fear, hate, Love, Peace, or Joy.

Non-Physical Players

This section can be a little tricky. It can push a lot of belief buttons your mind holds depending on the life experience to date. Some minds may have yielded enough to allow the entertaining of Non-Physical beings to exist. Some were raised with this knowledge. Still others find themselves thrown into it, ready or not.

Below I will talk about some Non-Physical players you may meet as you play The Game. I usually refer to them collectively as Spirit, Guides, Friends, or Mentors. The name is not important as it is a placeholder for those higher-energy beings that are not in physical form. This is not a complete list of Non-Physical beings we interact with on a higher level, but I think you will have your hands full with these players for now.

Earlier I spoke about how various topics, this book and your life can cause deep questions to come up. This topic around the Non-Physical players caused me to question the who, what, and why of these players in our life experience. This is how my Non-Physical Friends explained it:

Before this life experience, your Soul was hanging out with its Non-Physical Friends (Angels, Guides, Ascended Masters, and such). As everyone was hanging out, it was suggested to take a road trip. Your Soul agreed to be the driver of the vehicle (you, the avatar) and your Non-Physical Friends would be there with you, ready to give direction. They agreed to only step in when called upon by the Soul. No one likes a back seat driver, right? The road trip being this Game right now with you.

Imagine if you will, trying to drive a car that has a mind of its own and your Friends are in the back seat having a good old time waiting for you to ask for help. Yeah, that's The Game. And here you sit right in the middle of it.

You may have encountered one of these amazing Non-Physical beings coming through a physical player. I know you have met them. Those amazing folks who say just the right thing at the right moment and it pierces your heart in a good way. The essence of their words or actions stays with you and years later you realize that they were a guidepost, a sign to direct you to your Soul. They caused you to shift and it meant everything to your life experience. Yep, they were your Angels and Guides reaching out to you.

Let me introduce you to some of your travel companions.

Angels

This conversation can get deep really quick. For now, let's keep it simple. There are Angels. Lots and lots of Angels doing all kinds of things on many dimensions. Their Vibrational energy is only slightly stepped down from that God energy we are all a part of. Remember, Infinite Unconditional Love, Peace, and Joy Energy?

Some names you may recognize are Michael, Metatron, and Rafael. Let me tease you with the idea that these are the male aspects and Angels are both male and female, just like your Soul. Some of the ranking of Angels include Archangels and Seraphim. All are available to assist your Soul.

Angels cross many dimensions. They transcend the trappings of the mind because, well, they don't have an avatar to cruise around in. They are Divine Wisdom.

They have dedicated themselves to serving/supporting each and every Soul on its adventure. Some folks are able to see them, and some train themselves to do so. Or they, like me, have come to hear them, both clairaudient and vibrationally. We all have them. They are ever-present. Remember my analogy about taking the road trip. These are your party buddies who came along for the ride and are waiting for you to invite them in to help along the way. Their role is to steer your mind to your Soul. They help you to learn how to Trust that which you are and *feel* the Unconditional Love that is there for you and is part of you. Sometimes they will jump in and move something that needs to be moved but usually they are there to point the way and have a good laugh with you. Sometimes it will *feel* like it's a good laugh at you.

> They do that too, I'm sure, but it is with the limitless Love of God.

I recently had a conversation with someone who was sharing how Spirit put something in their way to punish them. NO! That is not how The Game works. We are talking Unconditional Love, Peace, and Joy. Spirit/God/Soul does not punish us or 'teach' us lessons. What we do have is free will and that just adds to the fun or complexity of The Game. Okay, just needed to be clear on this.

> This probably belongs in the Rules section too.

Guides and Ascended Masters

Probably the easiest way to differentiate Angels from the Spirit Guides and Ascended Masters is that Angels have a higher frequency or energy about them as a result of their proximity to God energy and are able to transcend the highest dimensions.

Spirit Guides and Ascended Masters have lived many lifetimes and have mastered The Game. They have transcended the mind and are able to create what we would call miracles because they are without the limitations of the mind. Insert "Dungeon Master" and discussion on clichés reference.

A number of Ascended Masters have come through to me over time and have helped me come to know my Soul in ways I never knew possible. To experi-

> In writing this, I could feel the flutter of my heart center. Did you feel it, too, as you read those words?

ence the essence of Love, Peace, and Joy and realizing that we have no way of conceiving of the infiniteness of God's Unconditional Love, Peace, and Joy.

Let me introduce my Friends and coauthors: Jesus, St. Germain, Merlin, Quan Yin, Lady Nada, Mother Mary, White Buffalo Calf Woman, White Tara, Melchizedek, Djwal Khul, and Kuthumi. This by no means is a complete list of AMs or Guides. Rather, these are the ones that have come forth through my work to guide me and have had a heavy hand in the creation of this book. They come together in a blended energy with the Archangels. My mind is wanting to jump in and explain more about these Masters, but for now I feel we will move on.

Other Avatars

All those people you see moving around you, family, friends, and those you have not actually met on the 3D board yet. All avatars playing their own game. Like you, they move around in their little bubbles of their own making. Sometimes we play a game or two with them and some we won't.

Helpful tips when encountering another avatar:

- You cannot create in another's game bubble. You may influence them by rubbing up against their bubble, but no one creates in another's bubble.
- No two avatars are having the same life experience.
- Life experiences color the way we see our life, kind of like filters on a camera.
- As a result of these filters/perspectives, no two avatars are seeing The Game board in the same way. Imagine over seven billion perspectives of the same game board. It is a miracle we navigate this game at all.
- It is important to know that you are not capable of knowing what is in another avatar's mind or see life from their perspective. Sometimes we *feel* like we can or should, but you can't.

- Some avatars have old Souls that have played many a Game and others have newer ones.
- Multiple Souls, Soul Families, and Twin Flames? Great topics for a deeper dive.

Rules of The Game

Avatar you have been taught to play by certain rules/laws while others were omitted. Let's discuss some of these.

- Rules that tend to involve limitations of time, abundance, age, education, and such are third dimensional. They began as a thought, then entrenched themselves as beliefs and social mores. These rules and laws are always changing and different based on where you choose to live in the world. They do not exist in other dimensions.
- You may not be aware of Universal Laws, which are completely different. These Laws are based on Vibrational energy. They don't change, are always in effect, and exist on all dimensions. Two very important ones to know are:
  o The Law of Attraction- Like attracts like. Your Vibrational energy attracts the vibrational match to that energy.
  o The Law of Focused Thought- You are creating whatever you put your focus on.

These Universal Laws are the basis for everything in the physical and Non-Physical. Put your attention on the thing you want and get in a really good-*feeling* place about it. Sounds easy enough, right? Learning how to finesse these Laws will make playing The Game a real (pardon the pun) game changer. In Part Three, I will talk more on how to integrate this knowledge into your game.

- You can't get it wrong. As much as we have been conditioned to believe that, we can't. It always works to our advantage, if we choose to see it.

Object of The Game

All game instructions include the Object of The Game. What is the goal? What is to be accomplished? How do you know if you have won The Game? When does The Game end? Questions that all revolve around the idea of what makes playing The Game all worthwhile.

I hope that in describing the Object of The Game, I answer those questions and color it in with a little shift of perspective. Perhaps nudging you to rethink how you come at your life or The Game. Are you done with having your life come at you? Do you want to take on The Game and really play it? Let's find out.

> I suspect that there have been a few avid game players who have stuck with me to this point and may be wondering what the object of The Game is.

What is the object of The Game?

First off, the goal is to have fun! It is a game after all. Lighten up!

I drive my family crazy by saying that on game night. I am usually met with answers like, "Only losers say that" or "I guess you don't want to win." Neither is true as they usually find out. Those are statements that shed a little light onto how someone comes at their life or how they are playing The Game. Can you *feel* the heaviness in those statements? Sure, they were trying to be funny, but isn't the adage; in every joke is a bit of truth? I play for the experience of having fun, win or lose and so does your Soul.

Often, I hear people say that the reason we are here is to learn lessons or our Souls can't move on. How about, our Souls need to clear their Karma or be healed? Does that sound like fun? Keep in mind, our Souls are here for the experiences and they play from a place of Infinite Joy, nothing more. Souls are not being punished and are most definitely not here to correct their wrongs. They chose to play The Game. Remember you can't get it wrong and neither does your Soul. More advanced Soul's just play more complicated games.

Maybe a more fun way to approach this game is to imagine these so-called "lessons" as puzzle pieces received by the avatar. Each piece gives a clearer picture to the level of Game being played by your Soul(s). If you Love to play video games, then think about video game levels here. You unlock new tools and super powers as you move to new levels gathering up coins.

What are you trying to accomplish?

Avatar, do you *feel* like you need to be accomplishing something? Then your Soul has a mission. Your Game can be all about figuring out what it is your Soul is trying to accomplish in this short life span it chose. Some may seem insignificant (which they aren't) and others grandiose and what legacies are built on. Don't judge yourself or your Soul. Remember, your Soul is coming from Infinite Joy and you can't get it wrong. Relax and allow yourself to have this experience. In Part Three, I will help you to begin this discovery.

Who wins?

Is winning The Game still a thing for you at this point? I hear your mind saying, "How do you know if you won The Game?" There is no win or lose here. I hear you. I hear you grumbling and groaning because some folks have that competitive edge. How's this? You will know how you are doing by how you are *feeling*. AAAAAGHHHH! I know someone just blew a gasket somewhere with that one. Take a deep breath and hear me out.

If you *feel* good most of the time, you are winning. How you *feel* is an indicator of how well your Soul is shining through your avatar. If you and your Soul have become best buds, you will be *feeling* lots of Love, Peace, and Joy in your days. You will *feel* like a winner.

When does The Game end?

For the avatar, when you draw your last breath. For your Soul? It doesn't. It is Infinite. Your Soul will choose another avatar somewhere here on Earth or who knows where. It may happen right away or not ever. There are many, many, many levels to The Game. We only scratched the surface with what I have covered so far. I know that on a certain level of your being you can *feel* how deep this Game can go.

PART THREE

Let's Play

———

Have you enjoyed Spirit's whimsical way of getting you to think about a new perspective on living here on third-dimensional planet Earth? Were you surprised by some of it? This perspective came to me over time through my spiritual practice. It was a process that took time. Small steps that sometimes seemed too small to matter and went no place, and then suddenly opened up to a new level of understanding that changed my life over and over. Let me reiterate, though. It took time. It took commitment at times. It took learning to Love and Trust myself. It wasn't always easy or pretty.

It has been worth every step. Looking back, I don't think I would have gotten to where I am now if I had known where this would be heading. It would have been too overwhelming. I know I am not done learning how to play The Game. I am happy that my Soul knows the way. I don't need to know everything. Just where the next step is. This book is one of those steps. One of many with more still to come and I Love that I get to share it with you.

Here we are. Our avatars sitting on the Start Space. Earlier in Part Two, you were asked to describe your Game Piece. Who are you, avatar? Stop in this moment and go back to that section on the avatar and look at who you are. Who is this avatar your Soul chose? After you *feel* satisfied with your description, come back.

Now, let's look at your Game Piece. Are you male, female, gender neutral, or other? What's your race? Were you born with special needs? These answers begin to show you the avatar your Soul chose coming into this game, like it or not. These attributes will influence The Games both of you enter into. These will be the filters your avatar will see things through. Sure, you can change some of these filters, but that comes later in The Game when you delve deeper into the beliefs you have, your ability to recognize these filters and consciously decide to change them. Reflect back on "A Cliché." Start general, and then with time, add deeper dimensions to your knowledge of The Game, who your avatar is and what your Soul is wanting to experience.

For now, humor me in the idea that your Soul did, in fact, know what this life would be about and actively chose to participate in This Game, at this time, and in this body knowing, full well what it would encounter, and that you would be sitting here right now, not sure what all this means. Wait. Did you *feel* that? There it was again. That *feeling* in your heart center and maybe a tickle in your body somewhere. Maybe thrill bumps? Maybe a fuzziness in your brain? Your Soul and Spirit are making themselves known to you, Avatar. How fun is that?

Are you ready to begin playing The Game in a more intentional way? Are you wondering what to do with all the information laid out about The Game? Wondering where do you even start with all of this? Maybe your mind has snuck in to say, "You don't have time for this. You have too much going on. Life is just too crazy to play games." If so, maybe revisit with the intro to the mind, because it will be always present and ready to jump in to convince you to stop. How do I know? Because that is how the mind works and that is how The Game is played.

Now that we addressed that little interruption ... Are you ready to begin?

Silence? Then you are ready to begin.

Where to Start?

It is hard to say when someone will begin their spiritual journey. It is a very personal and unique experience. It begins as an awareness. An awareness of You. Noticing there is more than one voice running around in your head. One *feels* good and the other does not. The journey has begun.

I want to make something clear as we delve into this. Being born into your life experience with 'gifts' is not the same as a spiritual journey or spirituality. I have met many people who have shared how they have had special abilities since a young age and yet their spirituality was fairly non-existent. Remember that spirituality is nothing more than a person's personal journey into who they are and what they believe. As a person unravels their spirituality, they may uncover some abilities, but those abilities are not spirituality. They are layers of The Game being played. Two very different topics. Spirituality is the practice of self-discovery. A spiritual journey is coming to know Divine Wisdom and Trusting in All-That-Is with all your being. It isn't a box you tick off your list. It becomes how you see your life and live your life. Your personal lifestyle that you intentionally create with your Soul.

As we begin our spiritual journey, we begin to play The Game from a slightly higher vibrational place. A higher Knowing. Not so physical, linear, and tangible. We go through a seeking period. We can't seem to read enough or attend enough classes. We find ourselves *feeling* our lives from a new place and sometimes that can *feel* pretty darn amazing compared to where we were emotionally when we started. Or it can *feel* like a lot of work depending on your life experience to date.

We are beginning to learn about life's higher meaning, that second level my professor spoke of. Sometimes seekers mistake learning about spirituality as being spiritual. Again, two different things. Spirituality is the practice of self-discovery. It bears repeating. Think of it like getting a bike and reading about what a bike is and how to ride it. You can't claim to **know** how to ride a bike until you put your butt in the seat and start to pedal. You can read about spirituality but until you begin your own personal practice, you don't **Know** spirituality.

And yet it will be your own personal spiritual practice, unlike anyone else's. As you begin to be more intentional about you and your relationship with your Soul, you will really start to play The Game instead of The Game playing you. Many students have described their lives as coming at them and not having any control over it. Your spiritual practice will show you the illusion. You were always the creator.

What does a spiritual practice look like? Get ready. A lot of people cringe when I say these words. Meditation and journaling. Yep. These are the foundations to a sound spiritual practice and a great way to see and learn The Game. Think of them as the doorway to The Game. It is how to become acquainted with your Soul and the other Non-Physical players playing with you. These practices are found at the heart of all organized religions. Did I just hear your mind start to chime in again? Assure your mind that you are just going to do some reading and you're not committing to anything right now. No need to get all in a bunch, yet.

The Art of Meditation

We have all seen it. The word meditation conjures up the image of a yogi sitting in the lotus position for days. Monks in caves for lifetimes. Worse yet, if you tried it yourself, you probably gave yourself a FAIL. I can hear the whining now, "Why is this so important anyway?" I hear you. I know firsthand the internal strife that comes with the mere mention of a meditation practice. I remember when I started and I have heard it from my students for decades. It's too hard. Too hard to sit quietly, too hard to find the time, too hard. I know. I know. I, too, struggled with learning how to meditate, what it was, why it was important. And why was it so hard?

With time, I discovered what meditation really is and what it can and can't do. I have been teaching thousands of folks how to successfully have their own meditation practice. A meditation practice is the spiritual journey. It is getting on the bike and going for a ride.

Let me throw this at you. Without a meditation practice, when will you have the time to sit and hear all that is in your head? Go ahead, guess. When you go to bed. That's right. Can't fall asleep because you can't quiet your mind? Time to think about meditating.

Meditation has been linked to a lot of health benefits. Thorpe and Dasgupta discuss 12 science-based benefits of Meditation as[3]

1. Reduces Stress
2. Controls Anxiety
3. Promotes Emotional Health
4. Enhances Self-Awareness
5. Lengthens Attention Span
6. May reduce age-related memory loss
7. Can generate kindness

8. May help fight addictions
9. Improves sleep
10. Helps control pain
11. Can decrease blood pressure
12. Accessible anywhere

Here's some food for your mind. According to Pew Research, 40 percent of Americans meditate at least once a week.[4] Additionally, Keely shares that of those who meditate, 70% have been doing it for less than two years.[5]

Maybe if I share what it looked like for me at the beginning, you will *feel* a little bit more relaxed. Roughly five years after 'the incident on the way to work,' nothing had really changed by way of a spiritual practice. I felt I was doing everything the way everybody said you had to do it. You go to school, you graduate, go to college, graduate, get a job, buy a big house, dog check, kid check, husband check. Not necessarily in that order. All of this was supposed to make you happy, right? But I wasn't. I was kind of curious as to why that was, because I was playing by the rules and I was not *feeling* that Joy inside that I was craving. I felt this void, a kind of emptiness, a hollow *feeling* in the middle. Like something was missing and I couldn't put my finger on it.

I had heard a lot about meditation. I heard a meditation practice helps with all that stuff. I wasn't quite sure how and it was a difficult decision. I was a corporate America, multitasker, Type A personality. The idea of sitting for ten minutes made no sense. I could get so much done in ten minutes. Sitting, doing nothing went against every fiber of my being. But again, I just really wanted to change whatever was going on in my life and find a happy place to be with it.

I decided to give it a try. I decided to start with guided meditations. I felt they would be a good way to distract my mind seeing it was not on board with any of this. I knew once my day got going, stopping would be really hard so I decided I would sit first thing in the morning on Monday, Wednesday, and Friday. I found that I would fall asleep during the recorded meditations and decided to begin listening to the guided meditations to go to sleep at night too.

After a short time, I realized I was enjoying the down time. The guided meditations were making me *feel* more relaxed as I went into the day and my sleep was improving. I was *feeling* better overall. I decided I was going to increase it to Monday through Friday and give myself the weekend off because my mind was still not quite sold on the whole thing. That's right, I was making compromises with myself. I would do Monday through Friday and for doing such a good job my mind gets the weekend off. It didn't take very long before I started realizing that by Monday when I'd sit down to meditate, my days were a little crazy, that over the weekend all heck was breaking loose. It wasn't going as smoothly as my weekdays were. I was actually happier and calmer during the week than I was on my weekends. I suddenly realized during one of my meditations that it was the meditation helping to calm things down. I couldn't ignore it. My mind did not want to give up the weekend. It still wanted to be in control. Light bulb moment. Meditation is the practice of reigning in the mind. Me and my mind had a little talk. I told my mind, "You know what? When you're on your own, things don't go so smoothly. We are going to continue with our meditation practice every day and smooth the week out all the way." That was that. I have been meditating ever since.

Now my practice has changed up over the years. I have experimented with different types of meditation. Each has its own strengths. Each day presents itself differently and I meditate accordingly. I choose the one that allows me the greatest amount of focus. When I say focus, I'm talking about being in the present moment. When you're in the present moment, you're not thinking about what happened yesterday and you're not worried about what's happening tomorrow. You are very much in your moment of what's happening right here, right now. In essence, you are gaining control over your mind and where it is allowed to go.

There are a lot of different types of meditations. Here are some to think about.

Mindful meditation- placing your focus on a certain thing. It can be your breath, focusing on the inhale and exhale. Another is watching your thoughts coming in, thoughts going out, and not engaging them. Counting is a way to focus too. Count up to forty without letting your mind drift off to what it thinks is important in the moment. Or focus on the sounds around you; a fan, birds, nature, water.

Mantra meditations, Transcendental Meditation or Metta Meditation- Metta are Love mantras. Transcendental uses ancient Sanskrit mantras. Inspirational quotes that really resonate make great mantras too. The focus is being placed on the repetition of the mantra, not as a memorized statement but really connecting with the words as they are spoken, *feeling* the words.

A **guided meditation** is probably one of the more popular meditations. It's also called visualization or imagery meditation. Focus is on the visualization of what somebody is telling you. Walking down a path, sitting beside a waterfall, listening to the water, looking at the flowers, smelling the flowers. You get the picture.

Chakra Meditation We have energy points in our body and with the chakra meditation, focus is placed on those energy centers looking to open, clear, and balance them.

Yoga in its traditional form is meditation, the focus being on breath and movement. Hatha yoga is very mindful of breath and movement.

The idea of meditation can be overwhelming. Where does one start?

- **Commitment is very key**. Start with a manageable plan. I did Monday, Wednesday, Friday. The statistic earlier was that 40 percent of the people say that they meditate once a week. Start with once a week. You can always build out from there if you want to.

    Commitment is key because your mind can be like a three-year-old where it will push your buttons, it'll nag and nag until it gets what it wants. And if you buckle, then it's twice as hard to sit down the next time. If you're going to sit, sit. If you don't *feel* you can commit to meditating right now, put it off for a month.

- **How long will you meditate?** If you are using a recorded meditation, it will be that long. If you want to try mindfulness or mantras, start with ten minutes.

- **Put it on your calendar**. I found it funny how busy I got when I committed to the Monday, Wednesday, and Friday schedule. Anything that is important for you, needs to be on your calendar to hold that space for you. This may have you question your level of commitment to meditation. This is normal. Push through the mind's rebellion and put it on the calendar.

- **Find a quiet place**. One with no distractions. When starting out, everything will be a distraction. Maybe a room with a door to keep you in and others out. Hang a Do Not Disturb sign if you must.

- **Find a comfortable spot** like a chair or lay down on the floor or bed. I know we see pictures of people in the lotus position doing their meditation or some instructors require certain seated positions. Not for this. The key here is to be comfortable.
- **Decide what type of meditation**. Are you going to listen to music or a guided meditation?

You've committed to the day, time, place, and meditation type. Now it's time to sit.

- **Go to your Do Not Disturb room.**
- **Set a timer if you *feel* you need it.**
- **Close your eyes.**
- **Take three deep breaths.** Taking nice deep breaths, signals to your body to calm down and your mind to focus. Most of us are running around on high energy and we're breathing from the tops of our lungs. We're in fight or flight mode and that is not healthy breathing. Sit and take three deep breaths down into your belly and then exhale fully. You may notice your shoulders drop as you begin to relax.
- **Now the practice starts.** If you are new to meditation, you will notice your mind get very active no matter the type of meditation you chose. Be prepared. **It will be active**. It may begin to judge or say: "Am I doing it right?" "I'm not doing this right." "Why are we doing this?" You start to get a laundry list of things you have to do right now. Cleaning the junk drawer becomes very important. All this is part of the practice. Remind your mind that you are going to sit for ten minutes and notice what keeps coming up.

Meditation is a practice. Each day is going to be different. Some will be quieter than others. Some days you're going to be just wound up because somebody just said something to you. Maybe you woke up from some crazy dream that's got your mind going in a weird direction. Whatever. It's going to be different that day.

Remember, meditation is all about focusing your mind into the present moment, observing where your mind is at. Is it hyped up or is it nice and Peaceful today? Is it happy? Is it sad? How does your body *feel*? If your leg is uncomfortable, stretch it, move it. If you're laying down, sit up. If you're sitting, lay down. Can you *feel* the air on your skin? Do you *feel* your muscles relaxing for the first time in years?

Not engaging, just observing it? Meditation helps us to activate the observer.

But sometimes we just can't seem to quiet our mind down. It is demanding our attention. Maybe there is something in your life that has your attention in a big way emotionally. Do you find yourself lying in bed until 3-4 a.m. because your mind won't turn off? Now it is time for your journaling practice to begin.

The Art of Journaling

Ahhh, the art of journaling. Journaling and meditation are quite similar, and maybe we will start there.

- **Health benefits**: Cambridge has found journaling fifteen to twenty minutes, three times a week will improve memory, blood pressure, mood, working memory, and your health.[6]
- **Helps to focus the mind and activate the observer**.
- **It is a practice**. Each day is different.
- **Best done alone and in a quiet place**.

- **Different types of journaling**: Free Writing, Dream, Gratitude, Doodling, and Automatic.

Journaling and meditation can be done on their own, but when they are combined, an interesting thing starts to happen. Each accentuates the other and your practice goes deeper into Knowing The Game. Before meditation, journaling can quiet the mind. During meditation, journaling can help to remember inspirational thoughts that may come through and may be hard to remember afterward. At the end of meditation, journaling can embellish the good-*feeling* emotions and thoughts in a more physical way.

My journaling story didn't involve the same struggle to start as meditating did. I really wasn't thinking about journaling at all, much less as a part of my practice. Yet, it turned out to be a very powerful piece of the puzzle. It was 2, maybe 3 a.m., and I kept tossing and turning. My brain just kept going over an incident that had happened that day. It was a deeply hurtful situation and my mind wouldn't let it go. In the midst of turning the scenario over and over, I felt the nudge to sit and write. I wasn't sure where that suggestion came from and I didn't want to get out of bed. Then I heard, "It's not like you're going to be sleeping anytime soon." I couldn't really argue with that rationale. I did want to get some sleep, and soon, because I would need to be at the office early.

Off to the kitchen table I went, sitting with pen and paper, and started writing about the incident. The writing shifted to other topics. It was almost like I was having a conversation with someone. Two hours and many pages later there was nothing left to write. My mind was quiet and I felt very sleepy and ready to get some rest. I slept surprisingly well and felt rested when I woke up.

That morning's meditation, the incident was front and center in my mind again. I felt the urge to write. I got my paper and pen and started writing. The emotions were different this time and the conversation went in other directions. When I felt like it was complete, I sat in silence for my meditation. For the first time ever, my mind was quiet and oddly content. So began my journey of understanding my mind and its role in my life.

In Part Two, I introduced you to the mind, one of the players in this Game. I suggested that it is very much like a three-year-old child. Now, you wouldn't yell at or ignore your child, would you? Yet we do it to our minds every day, especially when we try to meditate. We shut it down in mid-sentence and we have been doing it for so long, we don't even know we are doing it half the time. Journaling is the perfect medium to hear your child. The mind is very preoccupied with survival and can be very fearful based on the diet of thoughts it has been fed up to this point in life. Remember, it only knows the past and can be very fearful of the future. Your mind only wants to be heard. It wants to share with you those fears. Funny thing that happens: once it is heard, it quiets down and you *feel* a content *feeling*. Sometimes we *feel* that to have a spiritual practice, we need to stay positive and don't want to hear the fearful stuff. Listen. You must listen to what your mind has to say and what it has to say in its entirety. Listening to your mind in this way can be a little shocking, to see what it has been holding onto for many years. Mind you, we are not digging up stuff, just listening to what comes up.

There are people who have said to me, "Gwen, if I put it on paper, doesn't that make it so?" usually in reference to the Law of Attraction. No. What makes it so is those thoughts that keep playing in your head over and over and over. You cannot begin to change the energy of what you are attracting without knowing what the thought is first. Once you begin to know what's going on in your mind, you can start to change up those thoughts. And as you change up those thoughts, your point of attraction changes, and you begin to attract the things that you really do want because now you've cleared up the fearful thoughts that have kept those things from you. Whew! That is a big chunk of The Game right there.

What I Love best about journaling is my meditations get really quiet. My days get really quiet. Yours will too. It *feels* strange to not have that whirring of thoughts going all the time.

I hope you are curious as to what types of journaling there are. Below are a handful to begin playing with.

- **Free Writing-** I encourage all of my students to use this. It's simple and straightforward. Free writing is just like it sounds. There's no rules. You're just writing whatever's on your mind. Don't worry about the grammar, spelling, or punctuation. The focus is on listening to what thoughts are in your head in the moment and putting it on the paper.

- **Dream-** As it implies, keep your journal and writing utensil next to the bed so that you can record your dreams as they happen during the night or first thing in the morning.

- **Gratitude-** The focus is on things that you appreciate. Nothing will speed up intentional creation like gratitude. This is usually a natural progression for my students. As they move out of letting go of old thoughts they move into gratitude for the changes in their lives.

- **Doodling-** Focus is on the movement of the pen on paper. It can be landscapes, curlicues, or light and dark shades. Notice the thoughts in your head.

- **Automatic Writing-** Focus is on listening to Spirit and receiving inspirational thoughts. Conscious channeling, if you will. Recommended for students with a strong spiritual practice.

Starting your journaling practice is like starting a meditation practice. We can save some paper and ink by turning back a page or two and reviewing those steps. Again, I highly recommend that journaling becomes a part of your meditation practice. Make it fun too. Colorful paper and pens. A dear friend of mine uses spiral notebooks and decorates them with ribbons and photos. They are filled with lots of inspiration and gratitude. Yes, I am suggesting the old-fashioned type of journaling. No computer or phone. OK, I get it. It is easier, but there is something about putting the pen to paper and making it move on the paper that is mesmerizing, hypnotic, meditative. The action focuses your mind on the place that you're at and it allows you to move into a nice, solid practice. Besides, we are not looking for easy.

We have looked at how these two practices are very similar. However, they accomplish things in a different way. Meditation allows your mind to quiet so that you can start to hear that small, still voice. It gives us an out-of-body experience. Journaling is very physical. You're staying in the moment on paper, making your body move. Just one more reason they are a good fit for each other.

Final Thoughts

At the start of all this, I mentioned the nudges for this book have been coming for some time. I would make notes here and there and then it came to a screeching halt as I had family matters to tend to. Years passed. I saw an announcement in a group I belong to about a writing group. Some ladies, sitting on zoom with no audio or visual and writing. An accountability group if you will. I could *feel* the nudge to fire up the writing engines. Now I am actively writing this thing and I ponder it. I wonder about where it will go and if Spirit really does know what it is doing. It always does, but that hasn't stopped me from wondering sometimes. Over the decades, I have gotten somewhat comfortable with the bizarre happenings of life that are completely the hand of Spirit in action. I wonder, do most people have the same experiences? Who will read this? What will they think? Will they understand it? I don't understand it at times. It pushes my limits of reasoning. All the questions are flowing again.

This book has been flowing to me from Spirit and I have not been sure where it was going at any particular point. Sometimes the story would backtrack or jump ahead. A lot like our lives. Editing allowed for more information to flow in and be added. I had moments of doubt and sitting down to write was like learning to meditate all over again. This has forced me to organize my work, personal practice, and experiences for you, the reader, to understand and yet demonstrate through the written word what my journey looked like and to encourage you to follow yours.

During a particularly doubting myself moment, I came across a YouTube video which was an excerpt of Matthew McConaughey reading from his new book *Greenlights*.[7] I felt a nudge to check it out. I gave it a quick listen to see if it might be worth the read at some point. My takeaway in stumbling onto this video was how he had written it. It made me laugh. It may best be said that I felt a little more comfortable in the wackiness of my own book and the confirmation that he is most definitely one of my peeps. Again, just like life, it doesn't hurt to have a little confirmation when approaching new things and there have been a lot of them along the way.

I asked the question about whether or not, Spirit, may have left some things out? Yeah, the whole idea of this scenario we find ourselves in could be construed as a game, but does it all fit? There are some things in life that are just down right messed up at times and not at all "game-like." Explain that, if you will, my Spiritual Friends. I would rather not end this book more confused than when I went in, much less the reader.

Ah, the old multidimensional aspect answer.

Here is what I got in response to my most recent inquiry to 'The Game.' "Each person plays their own game. Games within games, if you will. Billions of games being played on this huge game board. Yet all of this is part of a bigger game."

Trying to take a non-linear concept and make it fit into a linear platform. From where we sit, some things won't fit. Our minds are linear. The questions aren't.

Remember the words from my professor at MSU? Three layers. First layer, each person playing their own game. Each gets to decide what games they want to play with others. We have the ability to move in and out of games. Some games are fun for the avatar, others not so much. Our Soul isn't judging. It sees the bigger game. I have outlined a way to begin to allow yourselves to view your various life dramas as games and learn to come from a deeper place within yourselves so you have the ability to walk away from the table and move to another game and find the Unconditional Love, Peace, and Joy that is your birthright and always available to you.

I listen, I *feel*, I flow with this life experience and yet the questions keep coming. They get bigger and bigger in their constructs. It is quite 'The Game.'

Book 2

Puzzle Pieces

——

There is more to The Game
than what you are seeing

Welcome Back

I ended the first book with a discussion on beginning your practice. Your spiritual practice of discovering who you, the avatar, are and becoming acquainted with your Soul and mind. Starting some type of meditation **and** journaling practice is key to the success of using these puzzle pieces and in discovering your own. I have had a fair number of students who felt they could 'skip ahead,' feeling they didn't need to have one-on-one time with themselves. I'll let you know now they had less than happy results and became very frustrated with the whole process. The information that follows will immerse you into a new way of looking at your life experiences. To read it will give you knowledge but without the practice to go with it, you will not understand it and this will cause a lot of frustration. Go back and review *It's A Game*, Part Three to explore a practice you *feel* comfortable with.

If you did begin to experiment with your spiritual practice, bravo. I applaud you full heartedly. I am very impressed with your commitment level to you and The Game thus far. Have you become aware of the two sides of you, yet? For some, this begins the journey to know more. This level is often referred to as the seeker level, an insatiable hunger to know more. You will seek out teachers and materials, experimenting with different modalities and belief systems. Some will resonate with you and others won't.

Shoot for the things that resonate in your heart, become familiar with this *feeling*. You are starting to have a conversation with your Soul. Learn to Trust that *feeling* and use it throughout this book. Your Soul will always *feel* good to you. It will always *feel* safe, warm and fuzzy. That is your Soul. I think it may have just hugged you. Did you *feel* it?

The more you learn, the more you will find yourself in life experiences that will ask you to commit even more to The Game. You will find your practice will be even more necessary to navigate The Game board. You throw the dice and start to move your avatar forward. Then you are faced with the choice to go left or right. It will look like the question: Do I believe what my soul is telling me or not? The answer to this question dictates if you will continue deeper into The Game or take a slightly longer route. Each time you encounter this question, you will find you have the choice to step blindly into nothingness in order to find everything or listen to your mind.

Drawing that line in the sand is where Faith steps in. Faith that you are Loved deeply. Faith that you are always supported. Faith that you are never judged. Faith that you can't get this wrong. Should your answer to the question, do you believe, be a strong yes, you move through that experience in a whole new way and begin to see life's illusion a little bit clearer, an Aha moment or a puzzle piece. A puzzle piece that lets you see the bigger picture of The Game you are playing. Some pieces fit easily and others you will need to play with before they fit. In the end, it will reveal a beautiful picture of the True you.

It is your choice. You can step back from the edge if you want. Have no fear, you will get another chance to choose soon enough. No judgment here. I have had many moments where I stepped away and later found myself exactly where I needed to be.

This book will be a little different than the first. This may *feel* more like *Hoyle's Tips on How to Play The Game of Life.* An insider's knowledge to let you level up your Game, maybe. I hope you have fun playing with these tips and are amazed at the level of manifesting you can conjure up by tweaking a few things in your life.

Funny, I tried to place them in a sequential order over and over again. I copied, cut, and pasted. Then I remembered our spiritual journey doesn't do that. There are no numbers on this path. My journey is different from yours and different from everyone else playing The Game. Some of us may find ourselves learning a similar puzzle piece at the same time and in the next moment we won't be. If your mind tries to organize these pieces and fit you into a schedule, let go of that notion. Don't *feel* you have to master all of these at once. Maybe read through them to get a *feel* for things and then play with the ones you *feel* drawn to. Each day of your life is unique and some tips will fit in this moment and others won't until later or never. This paragraph can be a puzzle piece for Type A personalities.

I am beginning to see that as this is coming together, these puzzle pieces can be used like oracle cards or a divination tool. What do I mean? When you are asking some big questions and need a little confirmation on what you *feel* is the answer, open the book to the page you are *feeling* guided to and let yourself sit with the message. *Feel* it. Does it resonate with you? Journal or meditate on it. Listen for guidance. This is the beginning of a dialogue with Spirit and your Soul.

Let's begin.

Puzzle Pieces and Aha Moments

We plop into 3D and keep wondering what this is all about. Why do so many things in life not make any sense? In spite of doing everything right, it all *feels* wrong. Sometimes we *feel* stuck for no apparent reason. So many questions and where are they coming from? Knock. Knock. Spirit calling. Yes, your Soul and guides are knocking on your door and you are *feeling* it. Those *feelings* push you to find answers and soon you are discovering your Spirituality. Gathering up Knowledge, a Higher Knowing. You are struck by Divine Wisdom and you find yourself with an Aha moment. A moment of complete Understanding. Knowledge that you may find hard to put words to or to fully communicate to another person. It will have a fullness about it. So much depth.

Aha! You have found a puzzle piece. I guess you could say I had a giant puzzle piece dropped into my lap that day in the car on my way to work. I have had many more since then. I will share some of them here for you. It will not be a full list and for good reason. **You** are playing The Game and it is up to you to make some of your own discoveries. I don't want to take all the fun out of your experience, but sometimes we don't need to reinvent the wheel either. Remember, the very act of questioning, reading, and searching is part of your Game that you are playing with your Soul. Let your mind start embracing this concept now and develop your spiritual practice of one-on-one time with your Soul. I know you can *feel* a little tickle in your heart center. I felt it as I wrote that. That *feeling* is a glimmer of your Soul peeking through. Give it a quick hello.

Over the past couple decades, I have hosted a discussion group called Art of Allowing. During our Art of Allowing group, we would share Aha moments because our minds tend to be trained into only believing what it can see, touch, and hear. It dismisses Aha moments. You *feel* it in your heart center, but your mind cannot embrace it from the third dimension. It quickly dismisses it as your imagination or looks for some kind of logical explanation.

When we take the time to focus on an Aha moment and embrace it, we let our mind become understanding of it, acknowledging and accepting of it. Suddenly your mind becomes more aware of those moments. It will start to look for those moments and point to them. Each week as people would share their Aha moments, in essence, they were retraining their mind into a higher level of Knowing and amazing shifts in their lives happened as a result. Sharing in a group like that offered the others confirmation of their moments. Many times, I would hear participants say that they didn't have anything to share and as soon as they heard others sharing, they suddenly recalled that they too had some moments of their own. Those moments are happening all the time. We have trained ourselves out of seeing them. Write them down and remind yourself of them often. I encourage you to make this part of your journaling practice. Can you think of any recent Aha moments? Take a moment and write about it.

_____

_____

_____

_____

_____

_____

_____

_____

_____

_____

_____

_____

Let's take a look at some of these puzzle pieces.

My Soul's Work

O ver the years, I have met the guides and angels that I work with in very unusual ways. I wasn't searching them out. They sort of made themselves known to me. One of my guides is the Ascended Master Djwal Khul a.k.a. The Tibetan. I'm going to give you a little back story on how we met to let you see how things can flow in your life as you are playing The Game. It is not so much that you will work with this Ascended Master, or any for that matter, just be open to how Spirit communicates with us and through others. A friend of mine came up to me at a fair and shared a book called *Ponder on This* by Alice Bailey. A channeled work of the Tibetan, neither of which I was familiar with.[1] My friend said that it wasn't a book to actually read, but rather to use more like Oracle cards. Essentially, I was to open to a certain page that I felt drawn to and read what the message was. She said her guides had suggested this and that the book was on loan. Over the weekend, I played with it and loved the messages so much that I purchased a copy of the book for myself. It was heavy reading and soon it sat on my bookshelf untouched.

One day during a meditation, I was receiving some inspired information, a download as some people would call it. I wrote it out during the meditation as it was so significant and I didn't want to forget the information. After my meditation, I sat marveling at the information that came to me and felt nudged to pull out my Alice Bailey book. I did and opened the book to the area that I felt guided to and lo and behold, there was the statement I had just written. I felt a warm, fuzzy *feeling* in my heart center and my brain tingled. I knew this was acknowledgment that I would be working with this Ascended Master. This would be the second Ascended Master I was introduced to and would begin to work with.

I was curious about who DK was and I felt I needed to learn more about him. I began spending a little more time with my *Ponder on This* book and some of the other books that had been published by Alice Bailey and a little digging into who she was as well. Her channeled work of this Ascended Master wasn't the easiest material to digest, but it answered a lot of my questions and came to be significant in my meditation work I would do later called the Heart Opening Activation Meditations.

I came to discover that my Soul's work would be the Antahkarana, or Rainbow Bridge. I would be teaching folks how to build a dialogue with their Soul. This puzzle piece was a big one for me about what my Soul's Work would be and for you, my friend, as you sit here. Let me explain.

Let's begin with the understanding that we come into this body still connected to the other side by a series of threads. The first is the life thread. This thread is intact if your heart is beating and your lungs are breathing.

Another thread comes through your Pineal Gland and is where communications from Spirit come through. Spirit, as in your Angels, Guides, and such. It can be vibrational or through one of your senses. You have probably heard of clairaudience or clairvoyance. I often am interpreting the vibrational message of spirit but on occasion have heard Archangel Michael getting my attention with my ears or smelling the perfume of a loved one or the touch of an Ascended Master during meditation.

The third thread is your Soul connection, located in your heart center. This thread is always open and flowing **to** you. You will *feel* it as Unconditional Love, Peace, and Joy. It is that resonating sensation you sometimes get when you know something is right. Your heart of hearts, if you will. Maybe you are *feeling* the thrill bumps now as your Soul begins to frolic in your knowing this, Truth.

As you travel your path of spirituality and develop your awareness and connection with your Soul, you begin to build a dialogue with your Soul and create an integrated personality that is the expression of the Soul.

Receiving guidance from your Soul is ever-present. Learning to ask your Soul questions and feeling the answers takes you to another level of being. The heart thread opens more and more, and soon your dialogue is a dance of movement in this life experience with your Soul. The separation of body and Soul fades.

How did this piece fit? If it didn't, set it aside for another time. Let's move on.

The Dialogue of Spirit

‎———

Some call it nudges, confirmations, or synchronicities. It will come as a warm loving connection in your heart center or goose bumps as you share something. You may *feel* a soft vibration in your head. Sometimes it's one or all these sensations. It is Spirit. It is your Soul connection and/or Universal Energies colliding in your physical beingness. Begin to recognize these, by whatever word you choose, as evidence of your awareness of being the conduit of Spirit in all its forms.

I love to share examples of this in my classes, groups, and talks as Aha moments. How better to learn than to relate to a story? I hope to share enough of these throughout this book to set you at ease. Some shares may seem a little too farfetched to be real, but they are. That is how I know they are True. I couldn't miss or dismiss them. Sometimes, those who were present in the unfolding quickly dismissed the happening. That is all right, as the message was usually meant for me anyway. Here is an example, in case you need one.

For a number of years, I could *feel* that at some point a book would be in the making. The avatar Gwen was not wanting to pursue this, but the nudges or pushes, as it were, were so strong I had to do it for fear that my body would start to do it involuntarily. Yikes!! Can you say out-of-body experience or trance channeling? Not this girl. So, I would write down the inspiration as it came through. Years passed and circumstances forced me to push it off to the back burner. Then one day, a lady from my women's networking group suggested starting a writing group. We would meet for a couple of hours on Zoom, mute our microphones, turn off the video, and write. I felt the nudge to say yes. I wasn't sure if I could just sit and write, having only written out of necessity. The first day was spent looking for my work and reacquainting myself with what I had written to date. The next time, I reorganized and added a few notes here and there. The next, the words started flowing and as each session would approach, I would begin to get 'downloads' during that day's meditation. Incidents would happen to support the story line and direction. For instance, the need to get the *Dungeons & Dragons* book.

As the book was getting close to being completed (so I thought), I began to get a little nervous about how one goes about publishing a book. I wasn't sure where to even start with the whole process. I told Spirit that I was going to need a lot of help with this. One day, I was visiting with my networking group and noticed that there had been a talk on tips for book publishing. I felt the nudge to listen to the recording and to follow up with one of the ladies on the panel. I went to her website and discovered the program she was offering, which handled everything about publishing a book. I reached out to her and the rest is history. The best part was she got my woo-wooness.

Building a dialogue with Spirit requires conversation. Not just asking or listening, but asking **and** listening. During your meditation and journaling practice, share what is going on in your life. Ask questions if you want and then sit quietly and listen. We sometimes think that if we use our words to ask that Spirit will answer in kind. Often, the answers will come as guidance in the form of a question. If you don't hear something right away, move through your day. If you *feel* a nudge, move on it. That is the dialogue of Spirit. Over time, you will develop your own communication and Trust in this Divine Wisdom that you are a part of.

Weak Links

What a great idiom. The weak link in the chain is what causes it to break. I like to use it to refer to our imaginary armor we put on. Life, up to a point, can be very painful and to protect ourselves, we put up walls or armor to keep others out. Spirit will use our weakest link or the chink in our armor to reach us.

My weak link is books. Spirit communicates with me through books. I have had books fall off shelves. They have hit me in the head with the title glaring at me and answering the very question I had. My publisher got firsthand experience with me and books. I have had friends show up saying their guides or angels suggested I check out a book. I remember sitting in the passenger seat of a car and pondering the big questions of life, only to see a car go by with the biggest book I have ever seen in the back window, shouting the answer at me. Yes, books.

Let me share this story.

One day, my daughter and I were sitting at one of Naples' infamously long red lights. The gentleman in the car to my left motions to me to roll down my window. You know, the old-fashioned cranking action that absolutely no one has to do anymore. I obliged him, and he began to tell me he had two books I needed to read. The first *Anna, Grandmother of Jesus* and the second book

I couldn't make out because my brain was still processing what was happening. My confused look caused him to repeat the books before driving away.

My daughter looked at me and said, "That was weird." Me, "Yes, yes it was, but momma doesn't need to be told twice." I searched out the Anna book and wow. I had out-of-body experiences as I read it. Past life regressions, my body completely vibrating, and more. Holy crap!!! Do I need to say I love that book? Unfortunately, I didn't get the name of the second book and I was sad about that.

Fast forward a year or so and I was the bookstore manager at the local Unity church. I closed the store and everything was put away and in its place. Next morning, I show up and there is a book lying on the counter. It was an older book, not something we were selling. Hmmm. Where did you come from? No one was on campus and there were only a couple of people with keys to the store. I asked around later that day about the book and no one had any idea of its origins. Of course, I knew it was a message from Spirit. I took it home and began to read it to see what message lay in wait. Not too far into the book, I began to hear, "I wonder if they have a website?" My mind was like, "Yes, I am sure they do. I am trying to read this book, thank you." Then the question came again and again. Finally, I stopped trying to read and set out to find the website I apparently needed to find. Did I mention that you will be sent on scavenger hunts with Spirit? No? I guess we have another topic to cover.

The voice was not clear as to whose website I was searching for and opted for the publishing company as I couldn't determine who the author was. Hmmmm. This company was not active and seemed to have published only a few books. Take a guess which ones they were? *Anna, Grandmother of Jesus* and the book I now had in my hand. I kid you not. The book I had in my hand, *New Teachings for an Awakening Humanity*, was a channeled book by the publisher of *Anna*. This book had been out of publication for years and it seemed pretty hard to come by according to Amazon. Crazy, right?

Oh, it gets better. I then told a friend about this and the name of the Author/Publisher, Virginia Essene. Turns out my friend actually knew this person in real life. She encouraged me to reach out to Virginia as she loves stories like this. I do write to Virginia and the only thing she is interested in is whether my friend is going to the upcoming Hathor conference as she needs a room-mate. What?

Yeah, welcome to my life. I did finish New Teachings and loved it. Both books are amazing. They shed a ton of light on what my soon-to-be spiritual work and life experience will look like. Never knew who the man in the car was. When it was done, I connected two old friends for a trip to the Northwest.

A puzzle piece for you may be discovering your weak link.

Who Are We?

———

S uch an age-old question. It is a perfect example of looking for a puzzle piece. This is a really big puzzle piece, too. It transcends the first two levels of Knowing. It is a third level question and there isn't any easy, quick answer that fits everyone's avatar. Each Soul is unique and each avatar is unique. Add to it that each avatar has a set of filters and beliefs acquired in a specific life. Reflect back on this discussion in the first book. Your Soul's answer to your questions will need to go through these filters to reach you. Some of us have some pretty dense filters preventing much of the response from getting through. The answers will have the flavor of the beliefs and the life experiences to date, leaving us with many different interpretations. The beauty of The Game is that there is no right or wrong answer. Only our opinion or judgment of right and wrong. Spirit doesn't judge any of this.

Thank goodness there are so many teachers with so many perspectives on spirituality. Over seven billion completely individual individuals and growing. Some believe in Angels, others in animal totems, and others are more science based. Some have shut the door completely.

Back to the question of who we are. Here is the answer that resonated for me. This one I am borrowing from an old teacher. Imagine with me that your body is the Universe/God/Whatever.

It is All-That-Is. The tip of your finger is you, the avatar. You are still part of the hand but the furthest most point of the whole. I have heard a similar analogy using the ocean and we are the drops of water. Either will work. I like these analogies because they can go deeper in their meaning as we go deeper into our Game.

We can dip deeper into this metaphor if you like. Just as your finger can touch and feel, sending messages to your brain, so do you. Avatar, you are God's ability to experience itself. To *feel* all the emotions that are here as we play this Game. The skin of God, if you will.

The answer that will resonate with you may not come right away. You may need to travel down your path a little further. This is not a gauge of spirituality. It is one of many puzzle pieces. If the question won't let you go, then ask Spirit to guide you in finding your answer. My answers, these puzzle pieces I share with you here, took years and years to come together.

If this resonates in your heart, AHA, you have found your puzzle piece. Let's see if we can build off it.

Road Trip!!

———

You may recall my road trip story from the previous book. It was an important Aha moment for me in placing the players on The Game board. Remember, this board game is multidimensional and our minds are not. Analogies help me to train my mind into a different framework when looking at The Game. I hope they help you, too.

This one came to me a number of years back when I asked, "What are the Angels and Ascended Masters all about?" That higher realm of energy that seems to make itself known to us. This is what they said using my college days filter.

One day, while your Soul was hanging around in the higher realms with its multidimensional Friends looking at Earth's many life experiences happening, it was decided that a road trip was in order. Your Soul agreed to be the driver and provided the vehicle (the physical body you are now in). Your Friends came along for the ride. They are hanging out with you right now. They agreed not to be backseat drivers. There they sit taking in this life experience in the higher dimensions, waiting for you to call on them to play The Game. They are here to assist your Soul and guide you to your Soul.

Genius, right? The analogy fits and resonated fully for me. Then I scratched my head and smiled, asking, how drunk were we? Why would anyone say, hey, let's get into a vehicle that has a mind of its own and won't listen to anyone or anything? I guess on some level it sounded and looked like fun. I'm being shown a rollercoaster right now by my backseat drivers. Be ready. Once you have invited them in, the fun really begins.

Maybe a 'for instance' is in order. I think I will use a more recent story, one that's pretty relevant to the whole moment for me. Recently, I was having a conversation with my publisher about the content editing and such, which was making me a little uncomfortable, when some books fell off her bookshelf behind her. She wrote it off as they had fallen because she had been moving books around earlier. We went back to the discussion and more books fell. She wasn't sure what was up with that. I explained that I knew exactly what they represented. Books are my weak link and Spirit was bringing to my attention the resistance I was having with some of the recommendations that were being made. Spirit was reminding me that she had published her own books. Note that all the books that had fallen on both occasions were her books that she had written. A week later, we were having another discussion about content editing, et cetera, when behind her again, all the books that she had written fell off the shelf. I wasn't sure why, as I wasn't *feeling* any resistance to the conversation. This time she laughed and said those were meant for her to remind her that I may have more than one book coming. Sometimes Spirit will jump in when needed.

You may have Spirit assisting in the most noticeable ways or not. Your Soul, Angels, and guides are always part of the experience. When we allow ourselves to be more open to The Game and the rules we are playing by, things happen in extraordinary ways. Synchronicities speed up, nudges have more relevance, and life becomes more fun. Did you *feel* any puzzle pieces in there?

Rationalizing

———

One may ask, if the Soul is so powerful and all-knowing, why doesn't it just come in like that? Why do we go through all of this having to remember who we are and how we are in the driver's seat in an environment that bends to our wishes? Wouldn't it be easier to come here knowing everything?

If we knew everything about everything, then we couldn't play The Game. It would be like watching the end of a movie first or reading all the spoilers on Reddit. You lose something in that. When we go through the birthing process and form our lives as babies, children, and adults, we are creating the "character" we chose to be. There are some variables that need to come into play, pardon the pun. Maybe think of it in terms of the ultimate Live Action Role-Play situation. How best to fully immerse yourself in your role? Like movie actors. Think about it. The best ones are those who immerse themselves in their character. It makes it more believable for the viewer. I love when I watch a movie and don't recognize the star. I think you are following me on this.

Another point to be made is each of us are completely unique in every way. Can you begin to see how very unique each of us is? No two characters are the same. Not on any level. We may flow from the same Source, but we are very unique as an avatar and Soul. That was factored into The Game. It isn't about coming in fully formed as a Spiritual Being. At your core, you are. Even the Ascended Masters had to navigate The Game of the physical world. It isn't a race to the finish and it isn't about everyone 'awakening' in this lifetime. Some Souls choose lives that will never do that. Some are new Souls to The Game and need to have some well-supported life experiences their first time out. As our planet ascends through the dimensions, some Souls hold the old energy to keep things from getting too crazy.

The planet continues to ascend through the dimensions and so do we. The planet ascends because of us. The youth of each generation comes in a little more in line with Spirit. I think we can see this in the blending of sexuality within one's avatar. Have you noticed the feminine and masculine characteristics are softening and the result is beautiful? Our Souls are not male or female, they are male **and** female. The higher dimensions also allow more and more avatars to be aware of their empathic abilities with little or no pursuit. Ready or not.

Maybe this life for you and your Soul is about determining who You chose to become. How far were You going to go with anchoring your Soul presence here? If you are reading this, I will guess your Soul chose a path of allowing the avatar to discover it in this life. Nothing more, possibly. How content can you be with this knowing? Is it your mind or your heart that is driving you? Can you *feel* your Soul nudging you now as you read these words? Can you allow others to be who they are without judgment? Sit with this for a moment or two and *feel* these words. This is a big puzzle piece to find a space for.

As Above, So Below

———

Universal Laws are based on vibrational energy. They don't change and are always in effect and exist on all dimensions. They are: The Law of Attraction and Law of Focused Thought. Below are very simplified explanations of each. Maybe you are aware of them. Now may be the time to be mindful of how they work. Book Three will go deeper into understanding these laws.

The Law of Attraction- Like vibration attracts like vibration. To better understand what vibration you have on a subject, look around. What does your life look like? How does it *feel*? Does it *feel* good to you or not-so-good? Good *feelings* pull to it good-*feeling* things. Example: if you *feel* down in the dumps about going to work, your drive to work and your day at work will be affected. Your vibration or emotional energy attracts the vibrational match. Conversely, if you wake up excited to get to the office, your day tends to be smoother. This is a very simplified explanation, but this is enough information for you to begin playing with. See if you can notice how things shift with the shift of your feelings on things.

The Law of Focused Thought- Whatever you put your attention on, you are creating. This planet, the people, and things are all the result of focused thought. Avatars have the same power of thought. Whatever you spend your time thinking about, you are holding that in your experience. Combine your focus with your emotions around that thing and you can pretty much guess what you are going to end up with and how quickly. Using the example above: you may be focused on not being late for work. You are very anxious about the prospect of being late. You have your attention on red lights. Surprise! You hit all of them and you're late.

There Is Only Light

———

I think we all at some point in our lives debate the existence of an all-knowing presence. Something much bigger than ourselves. Some folks embrace that idea and others *feel* this is all there is. Whichever choice you make, it will define The Game you are playing.

Many religions have come to define their interpretation of It and in turn define The Game you will play.

For me, I have found many names for the All-knowing. The All-That-Is, God, Universal Energy, and so many more. I *feel* the names are a placeholder for the Unconditional Love, Peace, and Joy I *feel* when I contemplate Its existence.

I sometimes *feel* comforted in thinking of it in anthropomorphic terms. Other times, as the vibrational energy that fills me with Unconditional Love, Peace, and Joy. It often resonates with me as Light, our sun being as close to an analogy as I can get. The warmth and brightness. This is my relationship with the Omnipotent.

Many times, I hear or am asked what about the Devil, evil, attachments, and such. How do I protect myself? I struggled with responding to these ideas. They never resonated with me. Should I believe like I am told that there are bad things out there to get me? No. I don't and won't. It is The Game I am choosing.

How do I explain the evil in the world? The wars and such? First, we need to remember who we are. We are an extension of what I have just outlined above. As avatars, we have the free will to dismiss darkness and choose other scenarios to play. Some scenarios have better outcomes than others. Second, the Laws of the Universe will bring to us anything we wish to resonate with. Third, there are a lot of avatars out there who don't understand The Game they are playing.

Remember, Spirit doesn't judge. It is all good. It is not real. It is slowed-down energy creating an environment to play any game you choose.

You have the power to choose what you participate in.

There is always light. The light, like the sun, is always present. Even on a cloudy day. Or better yet—I love this one—you never enter a room and look for the darkness switch. My friends, you have the choice and power to put your focus on the Light or to close the curtains.

This puzzle piece takes some time to work with. We have been exposed every day of our lives to the beliefs of others. It takes time to undo beliefs, especially generational beliefs in evil and darkness.

Cutting Cords

We make connections with people and things all day every day. We can call them connections, cords, or threads. Some are bigger than others depending on the history we have with the person or thing in question.

We can sometimes find ourselves holding on to things, people and places, and not in a healthy way. Sometimes there's an ex, somebody who's done us wrong and we just don't want to let go of it.

If you're holding on to an old relationship, an old car, an old home, you can't allow the new thing in. You can't allow a new place or a new experience or new people to come into your life when you are filling that space with something else that no longer serves us our highest good. Sometimes we don't realize we've created a cord. That's okay. Cord cutting can be very general in that regard.

Consider a cord cutting ceremony. It's a good way to let go. Rituals are an easy way to stay focused on what you're doing. Some things need a little more attention when it comes to letting go, especially if it's a relationship you've been in for a long period of time. Just a simple "I'm not going to talk to that person anymore" probably isn't going to cut it if you are thinking about them every single day. This can be as easy as during your meditation, asking

Archangel Michael to sever the cords that are no longer for your highest good. Or you may be interested in something more formal.

Keep in mind, this is not a vengeful thing. I am not talking about doing somebody in or hurting them. This is about allowing the highest good to be attained for everyone and everything that's involved.

If you are going to cut a cord, you need to stop putting your attention there. If it is a relationship, you delete them off your phone, do not connect with them on social media, and stop talking about them.

Practice putting your attention where you want it. On a new person, place, or thing. Start to create what that looks like for you. What type of person do you want in your life? What type of home do you want? What type of car do you want? I think you're getting the picture here but if you slip up, no worries. Start over being sincere in your letting go.

Be aware of where you put your focus and how you feel. Some cords detach quickly and easily while others may take some time. Some you are resisting may be for your highest good.

This piece may look like it fits somewhere but it may not. If it doesn't resonate with you right away, set it aside and come back to it later.

This Morning's Musings

———

The information for this book was very disjointed, like life sometimes, I guess. This is what came through this morning. I am sure it fits somewhere.

The Game. At some point someone, somewhere, will say it is a rather sadistic Game. Soul's taking over avatars and going through all kinds of crazy scenarios. All for what? Fun and entertainment for Spirit on the other side? I get it. I have had some events I would have never chosen for myself and seen some things that are not pretty. In fact, this is a question I have had with Spirit on a few occasions when I find myself fully immersed in the trapping of my mind.

From our third-dimensional mindset and depending where we are on our 'enlightenment' path, it is a difficult concept to get our minds wrapped around.

Our minds can convince us of the beliefs that we are being treated poorly, no one likes us, and so on and so forth. Let me flip this point on its head for the moment. I remember a story a while back, true story, about a railway worker who accidently locked himself in a freezer car. The refrigeration unit wasn't working properly but he didn't know that. He convinced himself he was freezing to death. He wrote a note to that effect and the next day he was found dead. Our minds are powerful things. Our

Souls are even more powerful. If we choose to be mindful of the thoughts and beliefs we choose, we begin to play The Game for all it's worth. The sadistic part of The Game begins to fall away and we find peace from within, allowing us to experience a joy-filled experience. We become the solution to the problem we perceive.

And isn't that the beauty of The Game? It is set up to be so real that we get lost in it. It really wouldn't be much fun otherwise. On this one, you will have to find your own way. You may need other puzzle pieces first before this one will lay flat. Once disengaged and seen through the eyes of your Soul and guided by Spirit, you really understand and ease into the journey for what it really is. You can't get it wrong. It is all good. You are always loved.

Deja Vu

———

This was very perplexing for me and I understand not everyone has these moments. This is for those who do.

Early on in my life I would have Deja vu moments. I would be in the middle of something and I could see in my mind's eye exactly how that moment would play out. Like watching a quick movie clip playing. Sometimes I could recall having seen it before in what seemed like a dream.

These moments didn't have any rhyme or reason, but I always seemed comforted by them. It made me *feel* like I was on track with something. I usually kept it to myself because of the weird looks I would get if I mentioned it.

Later in my life while my daughter was going through a health crisis, I kept having a lot of them. While she was in the hospital, they were almost daily. I was doing my best to stay centered in my connection to my Soul and Spirit, yet it was the most difficult thing I had ever had to move through. The Deja vu moments seemed to be an odd comfort in a way, but somewhat confusing because of their frequency.

When things settled down and I had time to reflect on this, I asked my guides about these moments. They shared that Deja Vu are the moments that my Soul looked at while reviewing my life for the 'road trip'. It is those moments that caused my Soul to choose this life experience. The Deja vu moments were going to happen no matter what I chose to do in this life.

If you have ever had one of these moments, stop and think about this. Really think about the circumstances that you found yourself in. Consider that your Soul chose this life specifically for those experiences. I believe that is why it is so comforting to us. We are, in those moments, the closest we can be to our Soul and seeing life through its eyes. Mind blowing, I know. Some of those moments are beautiful and moving, and others, not so much. The whole time your Soul was fully immersed in the experience and showing you how it would play out. *Feeling* the depth of an experience that will never happen again and can only be felt through you in that specific moment.

Funny Thing about Waking Up

In my line of work, I am often approached by folks who share how they are now 'awakened' or 'enlightened'. It is that exhilarating moment of Awareness in which the energy of Spirit floods in and through them. I love to hear their stories and how much they enjoy the feeling it brings. I understand how it *feels*. It is like the door has been thrown wide open and all that is left to do is sit in that glory. I, too, have and still do love to sit in that amazing *feeling* of uninterrupted connection with Divine Wisdom. It is amazing. My Heart Opening Activations range from ½ hour to 4-hour events, allowing participants to go deeper into their connection with Spirit **and** their Soul to build their dialogue with each.

I do want to make a few things clear regarding this awakening process. 'Awakening' is about the consciousness thread. Our connection with Spirit through the pineal gland. This is only part of the process. Remember the road trip. The energy flowing to you from this thread is the energy of Spirit/your guides, if you will. Most often this will happen before developing the dialogue with the Soul located in the heart center. This beautiful energy is to guide you to that heart center. The awakening process **isn't** about escaping the third-dimensional game board by sitting in meditation for many hours a day blissing out in an attempt to shut out the world. Even though the door may *feel* like it is now open, it isn't completely open and blissing out is like looking at the light coming through the slightly opened door of Divine Power and Wisdom and never stepping through it. The awakening process is only scratching the surface of that amazing energy of Love and Peace. Let me repeat: **from the third dimension, we are only scratching the surface of All-That-Is.**

As we sit and connect in a more focused way, we can learn how to bring Spirit/God energy into our daily life and begin to understand The Game our Soul is here to play. Part of The Game is about how to immerse yourself in the third dimension **and** be aware of who you are. Finesse this vantage point and all things are possible. The world becomes a holograph to play in and with. I love the book *Busting Loose from the Money Game* by Robert Scheinfeld. He does an amazing job of outlining The Game and describing the illusion of life from the perspective of money.

I know when spiritual awareness first happens, we *feel* that this *is* it. We have arrived. Nothing more to do here. Some newly awakened avatars have argued this point with me. No worries. All is good. Enjoy your moments. At some point your Soul and Spirit will be ready to get The Game underway again.

Are you curious how to play with what I am suggesting? Book Three will go into this in more detail.

We Can Recreate Our Past

What if we could recreate our past? Well, the first thing you would need to do is visit with your belief system or long-held thoughts on the topic. This may be tricky if you are used to telling your story over and over to anyone who will listen. Yes, start with not telling those stories anymore.

But that doesn't release the emotional vibration around your past, does it? Funny thing about holding onto a vibration, you carry it with you everywhere you go. All you need to do is stop and look at what is going on in your life right now, change up that vibration, and it will take care of the old stuff, at least until we tell our story again.

Let go of the story and clean up any lingering vibrations in the present moment and bingo, you have a whole new life experience to create any way you want. I hear you. I hear you saying, "What on Earth?" Here is my evidence that we can recreate our past and see the change in our present moment.

The Bookstore Order

Let's travel back to when I was managing the bookstore at a local Unity Church. A gentleman came in and asked if it was too late to place a special order for a calendar.

I explained that I had just placed an order for the holidays the day before and wasn't sure if I would be able to rush a single item in time for when he needed it, but I would see what I could do. Later that day, the order I had just placed the day before, arrived. How could that be? It hadn't even been 24 hours. I opened up the box and started pulling out the items to make sure that everything I ordered was in there. Yep, everything plus an additional item, the calendar the man had requested.

I had seen Spirit do amazing things before, but this one really was shocking. I called the gentleman and explained I had in my hands the item he wanted to order and he could come and pick it up at any time. When he showed up at the store the next day, he asked how I got it so quickly. I explained what happened, and he laughed and said, "No, really, how did this happen?" I told him it was a miracle, thinking he would appreciate the irony, being a chaplain and all. But he looked at me like I had three heads. He didn't understand any of what just happened and the fact that I even mentioned it could possibly be a miracle was beyond his wanting to believe. We just laughed and he moved along. I knew what really happened and I was very thankful to Spirit for watching out for both of us and that very special person who really needed that very special calendar.

Where's my ...?

A girlfriend shared this story with me because she knew I was the only one who would get it. She had just gone to the corner store to pick up something for her headache. When she got home the medication wasn't in the bag with her other items. She went back to the store. The clerk said she remembered her and did find the medication at the register and gave it to another employee to return it to the shelf. The clerk called the other employee and asked for them to retrieve the item they had just put away as the customer had returned. Later that evening as she emptied the previous bag, out falls the medication she had, in fact, purchased on the first trip.

Okay, think on these and keep in mind that in both instances, no negative energy was involved. No one got upset. In fact, not a lot of thought was given to the past or future. Spirit/Law of Attraction was allowed to do its magic. Consider what we could really do in our lives if we believed in the power we have in this game.

Remove the How

This tasty morsel has been shared by a few of my favorite teachers. I would hear those words and my mind would argue, "What do you mean?" I still tend to be a Type A personality. My mind loves figuring things out. Every detail. Remember, my mind was already rebelling at meditation and journaling. It was not happy about handing over its dominion on controlling my life. What would my mind do if it couldn't spend endless hours figuring out the 'how' of something?

What I discovered in my morning practice was, I spend a lot of time figuring out how something would play out, or better yet, how it wouldn't. It looked like this.

- How am I going to find parking at this time of day?
- I don't see how I am going to get all this work done.
- How is my daughter going to ___?
- How am I going to find the money for that?
- How the heck did that happen?
- How, how, how?

You probably have similar thoughts all day. Lots of them about everything. All of them carry a low vibration of energy. They are heavy with concern, worry, frustration, or fear. All less than happy thoughts. Enter the Law of Attraction. Those heavy vibrations of energy will not work in your favor. It is not enough to just stop having the thoughts if you are still *feeling* the low vibrational energy of fear, concern, etc., associated with the topic at hand.

In order to let go of the how, two things need to happen. First, one needs to be able to hear their thoughts. Yep, meditation and journaling are the perfect time to see and hear those concerns. When you *feel* that heavy *feeling*, write about it. Look at the words. Are you too caught up in trying to figure something out from a *less-than-good-feeling* place? If the answer is yes, meditate on it. Ask for support in letting go of that worry or concern. Second, you will need a good dose of Trust in Spirit. Not an in-your-mind kind of trust, but in-your-heart-knowing-that-Spirit-has-got-you-on-this. It may *feel* really small but that is all you need to start. By shifting your focus to thoughts of Trust that all is taken care of and you don't need to figure this stuff out or other comforting thoughts, you begin to *feel* the relief from the how. Begin to let yourself *feel* the relief of letting go of the how. Give yourself permission to let loose the death grip you have around that subject. You don't need to figure things out. You do need to find a way to *feel* the relief from those negative *feelings* that those thoughts are holding. Practice with the smaller things that aren't tied into every fabric of your being. Everyone loves to start with finding the perfect parking space. It is a great way to practice letting go of the how and Trusting that you are taken care of.

When we can let go of the how and *feel* confident that our needs are taken care of, we let Spirit get really creative with how things happen for us. I have tons of amazing stories about this but I will save them for another time.

May I mention? A dance occurs with your mind when faced with letting go of thoughts. Some thoughts we have held onto for so long that our mind can't begin to imagine what it will do without that thought or belief. The thought looks like this: if I don't have this to be worried, afraid, or concerned about, what will we do? It is ready to spiral into its "and we are going to die" scenario. Reassure your mind, everything will be okay. Letting go of worry, fear, and the like, will *feel* good and good thoughts and things will fill the space. Retrain your mind. Give it new good-*feeling* things to think about. Not over-the-top types of things but ones that give you relief from *feeling* bad in this moment.

Focus, Law of Attraction, and Spirit

"What you resist, persists." Maybe you have heard this saying? Do you understand its meaning? Whatever you are pushing against, you bring into your experience. What about the Law of Attraction? Like attracts like. Your Vibrational energy attracts the vibrational match to that energy. Different perspectives of the same force operating in your life.

When we are wanting something, it is important that we put our focus on it in a good-*feeling* way. The *feelings* you have will let you know if you are moving toward the thing you want. Be mindful of where your focus is, though. This trips a lot of people up. I have the perfect example of what my point is. Quite a number of years ago, my girlfriend and I were chatting and she said she had a question about the Law of Attraction. Her nephew was visiting and was concerned she didn't keep her doors locked at all times. His father is a police officer and mother a nurse and both keep the doors locked at all times. Who is right? I explained it isn't about locking or unlocking the doors, but rather the emotions around the action. Do you *feel* safe or not when you leave your doors locked or unlocked? If you are a fearful person, you can't put enough locks on your doors and windows. The point is learning to *feel* safe in your home regardless of your doors being locked or unlocked and noticing when you aren't *feeling* safe.

Another story to my point. Some time ago, I rented a space to hold my classes and events. On the top of one of the tall cabinets was an altar of sorts. Some crystals and such were available for use during my classes. I never worried about them being taken and they never were. Then one day, the space would be used for a big event and as I was cleaning up, I felt the nudge to put those things away. My mind instantly reprimanded me for not being spiritual and trusting. I chose to leave them be as I was not going to come from a fearful place.

The next day, a number of the items were gone. I sat with that. What happened? In case I haven't mentioned before, Spirituality is a very multilevel thing. It is not linear. Yes, there is the Law of Attraction, but there is also Divine Guidance that sees everything and how it will play out. I had let my mind control the situation. I probably should have noticed the difference in vibration between the loving and supportive "put your things away" and the *not-so-good-feeling* reprimand from my mind.

Here is the takeaway. Just like the locking the door scenario, your emotions will give you an indication of what you are attracting to yourself. But if you get the nudge from Spirit to lock the door, DO IT!

Notice also:

First level knowing: Lock or don't lock the door?

Second level knowing: How does it *feel*?

Third level knowing: What does your Soul say?

Scavenger Hunts

———

Here and there I have alluded to Spirit sending me on scavenger hunts. I get a nudge I need to do something. When I follow through, I find myself on an adventure. I don't know who, what, or where it is about but they are always interesting. I share these notables to show the fun you can have with Spirit.

"Things that make you go Huh for $2000 Alex."

The first involved me getting a nudge to go to a popular yarn store. I love to crochet and the nudge to shop for yarn was exciting. Spirit thinks I need more yarn, yay! Off I go. I find myself wandering and not seeing anything I like. A woman approaches me and suggests I go to a local yarn shop that I was not aware of. I *feel* a nudge and off I go again. I wandered the store, wondering why I was sent there. Not really seeing or *feeling* anything, I leave. As I am heading out of the lot, I get a phone call that forces me to park in order to address this person's needs. I finish my call and look up to see I am sitting in front of a resale shop. Humm. I don't recall seeing this shop before. I *feel* a nudge and in I go.

A few years earlier in Michigan, I rented a space in a little shop and sold my crocheted items and other projects I loved to work on. I loved that space. I had secretly wished that there was a place like that in Naples. And here it was!! As I explored the shop, I met a lady who also crocheted. As we chatted, I discovered that she knew of my Art of Allowing Group and also loved Abraham-Hicks. She shared the ins and outs of the location. It was a beautiful journey and I was able to lay to rest the yearning to find a place to sell my wares.

The second notable scavenger hunt occurred in November of 2011. I was putting the finishing touches on the Follow the Light Tour that would pave the way to Spiritual Communities Network. The nudge came to visit a local spiritual shop. I had become friends with the owner and had done some work there and welcomed the visit. My friend asked what I was doing and I explained. She understood. She pointed out there seemed to be another person doing the same thing. We laughed and not *feeling* any nudges, I left. Later my friend called to tell me she had a conversation with the other lady who, in fact, was doing the same thing as me. She told her about me and the upcoming event and the lady wanted me to call her. I did and we talked about a host of things. Right as we were ending the call, I casually mentioned, the only thing remaining for preparation for the event was a graphic for the cover of the Directory we would be handing out. My new acquaintance laughed; did she fail to mention she was a graphic designer when she wasn't doing her spiritual work? We both laughed as we had discovered the reason for our connection. She was able to create a beautiful graphic and our original logo. Two people following their nudges so the work of Spirit could be complete.

One more for good measure? I was driving home one day and felt a nudge to go to Pier One. I wasn't sure why I would be nudged there but knowing better than to argue with Spirit, I went in. I felt nudged to the far corner in the back of the store. As I approached, I shook my head. We had recently moved into our new home and had decided to do the family room in a cinema theme. In front

of me, in the clearance bin, were two film reels to hang on a wall.
Exactly what my husband had suggested.

Beliefs Are Thoughts
We Keep Thinking

"Beliefs are thoughts we keep thinking" struck me like a bolt of lightning. I had heard that phrase on so many occasions by Abraham-Hicks, in their books, at their seminars, and on their CDs. It was one of those statements I would give a nod to but not much thought. I was focused on so many other aspects of spirituality. Apparently, my mind was not ready to embrace this concept in its entirety. Right now, it may be the same with you. No worries.

However, if your interest is suddenly piqued by these words, then you are ready. As I said, it was like a bolt of lightning for me, not a light bulb moment, if you know what I mean. More like the V8 moment. The depth of the sentence became so clear to me. How could I have missed this? Stick with me on this one.

All the spiritual teachers, in one way or another, comment on how thoughts are things, the power of positive thinking, and more. The focus is on the thoughts we hold and the idea that we can change our thoughts. Genius, right? Start changing your thoughts and things change. Throw in the Emotional Guidance Scale and you begin to see how powerful thoughts can be in the creation process of your life.

But what about the beliefs angle and how do thoughts tie in? Get ready, this will be stupid simple. Pick a belief. Any belief. Let's pick one. Mondays suck. Short, sweet, and a lot of people believe it. Mondays suck is a thought. A thought we keep saying and thinking, so much so that it is now our belief. We have evidence to prove it. Yet, this belief is nothing more than a thought we keep thinking, which means we can change it at any time and begin to see the evidence of it.

Ahhh, but what about those beliefs that our families hold on to, or our culture, or our religion. We put a lot of faith in those beliefs. We have invested time into them. People have died because of them. And yet, they are nothing more than thoughts we choose to keep thinking and let have power over our lives.

Even after the light bulb goes on or in my case the lightning strikes, it is not an easy puzzle piece to use. Even if you can point to a belief you want to change, some of them are wedged in so tightly, when you pull it out it brings some other stuff with it you may not be ready to undo just yet. Give yourself the time to explore.

Initiations

E arlier I mentioned commitment moments. Many would call them initiations. Initiations are the passing from one awareness level to another on your spiritual journey. Or leveling up on your game. They will have different emotional *feelings* associated with them depending on the level you are leaving. Some will be ecstasy while others may *feel* like the grief you *feel* when someone you love suddenly transitions from their physical body. These initial *feelings* of an initiation are temporary as you adjust to this new level of knowing.

Things to know about going through initiations.

Right before you slip into a new level of knowing you may *feel* that you aren't doing something right and fear you are going in the wrong direction. You ask yourself what you are doing wrong. Yep, that *feeling* is when you're on the cusp of something big that's about to emerge in your life. You may resonate with this now or not. One thing is for sure, you will forget this particular nugget right when you need it most. Unless of course, you are channeling me. A few of my longtime friends call them Gwenisms. Lol

How do I know this is Truth? Experience. Once you have moved into a new level of knowing, you cannot undo it. You won't lose this level of knowledge as you have passed through a Ring Pass Not. The Ring Pass Not is the Law that governs the initiations. A student cannot pass to the next level until they have achieved a certain level of knowledge. I am not referring to mental knowledge. A student/seeker will need to demonstrate and commit to their Soul/Spirit to achieve a moment such as this. This new knowledge will break down part of the illusion of The Game.

How many initiations will you go through? Depends on your Soul's agenda for this life experience. Some are on vacation and playing the awareness game is not The Game they are about this time around. Others want to play the Lightworker Game; that can be one very interesting ride. Just look at what you are reading now.

Holding onto Stuff That Doesn't *Feel* Good to You

————

Don't let all this scare you. As I mentioned, you will encounter initiation moments when your Soul *feels* you are ready. You are ready because you have put into practice the things you have learned. You now find yourself in higher dimensions of vibration. Things seem to be moving quicker. It doesn't take much to see the results of your focused attention. Your dialogue with Spirit is being fine-tuned.

As you move into higher levels of Knowing, you are not able to go back and play like you are ignorant of the new rules. You will need to play by your new rules of The Game, like it or not. The path seems to narrow and not allow for the free will thing you used to use as a weapon.

It is like having insider knowledge. Ring Pass Not, remember. Communication with people not on the same level as you will become difficult and you lose the luxury of holding onto things that are not uplifting.

You can try, but you will *feel* the rub. Your body will show the stress.

I like to use this analogy. Think of some of the thoughts you have that don't *feel* good to you. Imagine they are rocks in your pockets and your vibration is a lake. When you start your spiritual journey, you are up to your neck in this water. You move slowly. The rocks are light. Now as you begin to raise your vibration, you are stepping out of the water. The shallower it gets, the quicker you move, the heavier the rocks. By the time you get to the shore, the weight of the rocks is unbearable.

As you raise your vibration, you will *feel* the rocks. When you do, it is time to let go of them through meditation, journaling, cord cutting, or any other ritual you choose to dissolve the rocks.

You Can't Get It Wrong and It Is All Good

———

I don't think it matters when I put this piece in. This one comes up over and over again. Each new level presents a new set of circumstances to reaffirm to yourself that you can't get it wrong and everything is working toward your highest good. Easy to read. Not so easy at times when The Game gets down and dirty on some topics. We can convince ourselves we have done something wrong. If we used the right words, smiled more, loved more, created more vision boards, meditated more. Okay, we can always meditate more. Teehee. Yet even if you didn't, you didn't get it wrong and the outcome isn't bad. The Game doesn't work that way. There is no right or wrong, good or bad. There are better *feeling* outcomes to things, but it doesn't mean you got it wrong. You most certainly will NOT be punished for the things you did. Our minds are the only ones with judgment.

On those higher dimensions, our Souls, Spirit, God, you name it, knows exactly what is going on at all times, the outcomes of our every move way before we even thought about it. Like our GPS, Spirit hits the rerouting button and you are given another way to get all the good things if you want them. Like your GPS, there are many routes to the same destination. You get to choose it and your Soul helps you get there in one piece, if you let it. Even if you show up a little rough because you wanted to do it your way, it all still works to your favor. Always. I hear you. This is a toughy.

Spirit counts it all good. Can you *feel* that?

Ease up on yourself. Sit back and relax. Maybe do a little meditation and plug in some new destinations with a scenic drive.

Are You *Feeling* the Roller Coaster Ride?

———

A s you read these three books, you may begin to get the *feeling* it took a little while until I finally committed to my practice and you would be right. It took years for me to put things together and make sense of it.

I was so up in my head about everything it took a while for me to even notice the roller coaster ride I was on. When I was learning about spirituality and doing my best to do what everyone said, I *felt* good. Then I would stop. I would get lazy, not realizing that every time I stopped, I slipped back into my bad habits of thought. I would find myself at the bottom, each time *feeling* worse and worse. I would begin again, climbing to the top of the highest point I could reach. The ups and downs were rough.

Finally, it was commitment time. Either I believed what I had been learning or I didn't. I had to stop playing around with it. Commit I did. This needed to be a lifestyle change for me. The rest is history. I began my meditation and journaling practice. It was a slow go, just listen to my talk on starting a meditation or journaling practice but I stayed the course. Life began to level off. Life seemed to be less dramatic with those highs and lows. Things happened, but they didn't drag me down the way they used to.

Stop and think about your life in this moment. Are you *feeling* like you are on a roller coaster? You don't need to be. You just need to love yourself enough to start doing things a little differently.

You Can't Get Rid of the Mind

This may be a duh moment but I am going to say it anyway. Early on in my meditation practice, I got it into my head that if I was trying to quiet my mind, it must mean I need to get rid of that little booger. It felt bad to listen to. It got me into trouble all the time. It was unruly. Lots of the teachers at the time seemed to give me the impression that we need to get rid of it.

That was a no-win situation. I struggled with my mind on many levels daily. I was so frustrated. Then at some point during my meditation, I realized that I can't get rid of my mind. Spirit explained how our mind is a part of The Game. It is what anchors our Soul to this planet. It is useful at getting things done. I felt the relief in that message and began a new relationship with my mind. Understanding it and loving it.

Our meditation and journaling practice is designed to learn to take back control from it. To learn to listen to what it is saying. To learn to listen to the other half of ourselves. To integrate ourselves.

I forget this lady's name; she had a great analogy for the mind. She would envision her mind as a cat on her lap. She would pet it and talk to it. She would love it. She learned not to let her cat make decisions for her. I think this is the perfect relationship to have with our minds.

Unconditional Love

I have saved this until the end. It is a hard piece of the puzzle to share. I'm not sure where to start and my Angels and Guides are remaining quiet. They want me to speak from my heart, from my Soul. Some puzzle pieces are so big and touch us at our core. Especially if it is one that we seemed to have spent our lives discovering. A piece that transforms us. It transforms how we see ourselves and how we relate to the world around us. My dance with Love did that. I have come to find that Unconditional Love is the undercurrent of The Game. How could it not be? God is Unconditional Love, Peace, and Joy and this is The Game of that energy. Easier to read the words and agree with them than to fully *feel* the deep meaning of those words.

We come into the 3D being told who and how to love. We learn from those who really don't understand it for themselves and send the rest of us on a lifelong journey of searching for it in all the wrong places. Yes, just like the song. Some who do try to send you in the right direction tend to leave out some very important puzzle pieces of how exactly we do that. We run around with our goody bags grabbing whatever fits or appears to and hope for the best.

This puzzle piece is more like all the outside pieces. It is easier to build your puzzle when you get the outer edge in place, but it may not happen like that. You may find a corner piece and build the corner. As avatars, we are able to love each other. Notice the small 'l'. The love between avatars is wonderful. Yet for some, it is not the Love we long for. Do you *feel* this way? Stop and think of the relationships you have. Are they fulfilling or do they leave you wanting?

My father passed away when I was five and I spent the better part of my life trying to earn my mother's love. She didn't offer it freely, if at all, and I felt I could win her love and acceptance somehow. As a child I felt I must be doing something wrong. It hurt. A lot. It seemed the conditions for her love were always changing. In the midst of my spiritual journey, I began to Love myself. I developed boundaries with my mother. Then one day during a meditation, I was asking for guidance regarding this painful relationship I had with my mother. Spirit spoke to me. Stop demanding love from a person who is incapable of giving you the Unconditional Love you crave. I felt that to my bones. I was. I was demanding something from someone that couldn't love me like that. I felt the release of the pain, the relief, and I remembered that day in the car. Remember the day Spirit got my attention in a big way while driving to work? The day Spirit told me this was a game? I also revealed my walk-in experience. In that experience, I felt Unconditional Love, Peace, and Joy. The absence of judgment was striking. I now understood that there wasn't any way on this planet I would find that in another person. That level of Love, Peace, and Joy resides within each of us. Our Soul, the extension of God's Love, Peace, and Joy. It is not enough to mentally know this but to truly *feel* it for ourselves. The reason it took so long for me to understand was due to my beliefs. How could a mother not have boundless love for her child? I first had to untangle the web of a narcissist. Creating healthy boundaries and learning what Loving myself really meant as an avatar before going deeper into my heart. The more I discovered the falsehoods I had been fed over my lifetime, the more I felt my heart open. The more my heart opened, the more I discovered my Soul.

Are you longing for Unconditional Love? If so, you are in search of something that doesn't exist in another human being. Avatars are egocentric. They have to be for survival in The Game. Don't get me wrong, there are some really loving people on this planet, but the love you are looking for comes from within yourself and not someone else. Stop looking for your twin flame or soulmate. There, I said it. Learning to Love yourself and feel that Love that is there for you has been said a million times in a million different ways. Yet we continue to search for and demand Unconditional Love from those around us that are incapable of providing it. This can be so freeing in a lot of different way on so many levels. I hope this helps.

Trust

———

Run away from anyone who professes to know everything and keeps you from exploring your own personal Truth. Don't worship anyone. The only power they can have over you is the power you give them. To avoid this trap, practice Self-Love and Self-Care at your Soul level. Your Angels, guides, and Soul is where you place that level of Trust.

Trust. It's hard to say exactly when this puzzle piece will show up, but it will show up as you develop your dialogue or relationship with your Soul. Ultimately, as in all relationships, you want to establish a level of trust. Most of us trust people, and sometimes we find that some are not as deserving of that trust. We eke out a way to navigate a level of trust with the other avatars in The Game.

Unlike third-dimensional trust, Trusting in Spirit takes on a whole different meaning. It is the thing that will help you to navigate The Game and move through it effortlessly with a sense of peace.

Let me make a point here. Sometimes people get a little confused regarding spirituality. Some believe or are taught that as you become more spiritual, you won't have 'things' happen in your life experience. That being spiritual somehow exempts them from what some may call bad experiences. That is very far from the truth.

Rather, spirituality helps us to move through those moments with strength and courage, to face the situation in Peace and Love.

As you develop your dialogue with your Soul, an internal conflict will begin. Your mind deals with what it can see, touch, and smell. It only knows the past. Go back to Book One and review the mind and some of the tips I gave you there regarding the mind. Refresh yourself on that because it's important. When you're developing your dialogue with your Soul, your mind will take issue with what you are doing. Your Soul will inspire you to go in directions that will not make sense to your mind.

For instance, you may be *feeling* guided to turn left at the stop sign instead of turning right, which is the way you always go to get home and is the shortest route. But Spirit knows that it may be safer for you to go left or that you will encounter somebody you need to encounter. It's trial and error learning to Trust your Soul.

Start small. Start with things of little consequence. If you *feel* like you should go left, go left. Try it. See where it goes, see where it takes you. Reflect back, you may recall times when you felt guided to go in one direction versus another, you dismissed it, and the next thing you knew, you wished you had followed that direction. Remember my story about not going to the funeral?

Here is an example of this that I like to laugh about. Not too long ago, I was attending a fair out of town and was staying at a hotel for the night. The room was on one of the higher floors at the far end of the floor from the elevators. I was preparing to leave and the plan was to take all my bags, go downstairs, check out, have breakfast, and leave. As I was grabbing my bag and getting ready to go out the door, I could *feel* Spirit saying, "Leave your bags." I was like, "No, I'm going to take the bags with me." I felt this nudge to leave the bags. My mind said, "The room is at the far end of the hall from the elevators. You don't want to walk back and forth and up and down. Save yourself the time." My mind won that argument and I set off for the elevator. The elevator closed in front of me and as I was waiting, I could hear the people in the elevator talking. I thought it was strange that I could hear them talking. Turns out they were stuck in the elevator. The elevator was not moving and they were discussing how to get out of the elevator. I was happy that I wasn't in the elevator, but I also realized that if I was going down to breakfast, I would have to carry my suitcases down the stairs to the first floor. Ugh! So back to the room I went to drop off the bags. I had gotten a heads-up, but totally disregarded it. It's little moments like that where I remember I really do need to Trust Spirit, even in things that look pretty mundane and of no consequence because they are of consequence. Spirit knows the consequence in a far-reaching way and your Soul and guides are able to help you navigate through in the most efficient and helpful way. In fact, to this day, if there's a moment where I *feel* I want to go against the suggestion being made by Spirit, they quickly remind me about the suitcase incident and that's usually all it takes for me to rethink my thoughts and do what they suggest.

It always turns out fine, always. Play with this puzzle piece. Spirit will take care of you and it will have your back with Unconditional Love.

Spirit's Contradictions

I like to call these examples contradictions. This is when I began to *feel* like I was somehow seeing things from the other side. Let's give them a try.

- The expansiveness of who you are is not outside of you, but inside.
- We *feel* we need to protect our hearts. We suffer losses and the mind decides it will protect the heart from that pain by building a wall around it. Unfortunately, that wall cuts off our connection to our Soul thread. It becomes harder and harder to *feel* the guidance coming through. Our power is in leaving our heart exposed and listening to it. The pain comes from locking your Soul away.
- Wonder if you are connecting with Spirit? When you get an inspired thought does your mind tell you it's your imagination?
- If you want the big things, you have to do the little things. Ten minutes of meditation when you *feel* you don't have the time will open up time in your day.
- Appreciating the dime you found, allows the new client to show up.
- Big questions with small answers that turn out to be huge answers to small questions.

Feel free to add your own observations to this page to remind you.

_____

_____

_____

_____

_____

_____

_____

_____

_____

_____

_____

_____

_____

BOOK 3

Your Soul Connection

——

Creating an Integrated Personality

Living from the Soul's Vantage Point

———

Your *Soul Connection*, the third book to the trilogy of *Insights & Illuminations* delves deeper into the topics I touched on in the first two. My intention is to go beyond most social mores and take you, Avatar, into thought-provoking areas that cause the mind to expand and consider what lies below the surface of what we have been taught. Be ready to move closer to finding the answers to the big questions hanging in the periphery of the mind. I have learned a great deal over the years and I love to share that, Knowledge. However, I do not hold myself out as the one and only source of this Knowledge. The information I share only begins to scratch the surface of Divine Wisdom and what each of us can access on our own. It is not work to be taken lightly. It is not for everybody. My tone may seem more serious and to the point at times.

My method of teaching is different from most. Some students expect to be told what to do and think. The closest I get to that is encouraging a strong meditation and journaling practice. Those same students would take issue with my class structure, or lack of it. The structure is in the student in front of me and what their questions are. I listen to guidance from Spirit and my Soul to offer Insight into what their Soul is wanting them to Know. Each of us is so unique in who we are and what our Soul's intentions are; one size fits all doesn't always work. We discover Our Truths by living our lives. What we are experiencing in the moment is the Truth we are coming to know. Everything else falls away. If you *feel* this book lacks structure, consider where you are in this moment and what you are hoping to find. Allow yourself to flow with the words and the intention I am holding for you.

Right now, you may *feel* as though you are being pushed to move forward. Yes, the nudge you have resisted for some time may have become more forceful now, so don't delay. By all means, read on. There will be morsels that your Soul is wanting you to explore. I will be sharing with you, techniques to begin living from your Soul's intention and beginning to create an integrated personality. This process is not one that can be learned over night and some students have found they needed the support and guidance of someone who understood them because their life was a journey unlike any they had imagined. This book, *Your Soul Connection*, will get you started in understanding the process. Should you feel a need to explore further, I have provided information in the back of the book. As you start reading this book, it might *feel* a little like a refresher course of what I touched on in the first two books, but I hope to present it in a way that will speak more firmly to your Soul so that you may *feel* its presence and the depth of my words.

The Third Level of Knowing

Remember our guides are ever-present and always available. They agreed to play here in the third dimension with you. I am moved to tears as I can *feel* their presence fully as we start this discussion. They are rejoicing in this moment of being with you. We want to share with you a fundamental Truth. One you may not have considered, or possibly, were taught to the contrary.

It's a Game!! Until I heard those words, I was asking a lot of questions and *feeling* like I wasn't getting any answers. That day sitting in my SUV driving to work, I demanded an answer and I got one. My answer cut across so many levels of my Knowing and being. First, who were the voices that I heard so clearly? I was able to pin down that they were all crossed-over loved ones. How was it possible to hear them so clearly?

Second, It's a Game? What Game? It resonated in my heart, but its meaning at the time was somewhat lost to me. My life is a Game? For who? Books One and Two outline what I came to discover over the years.

Third, there was that other "person" who was in my body with me. A being that I could *feel* Unconditional Love, Peace, and Joy radiating from. A blending of these emotions that goes beyond physical understanding. I could sense it taking in my life in that moment. Not judging in any way. Even when it mentioned, 'This won't do,' there was no *feeling* of judgment. Only more Love, Peace, and Joy. All this caused my senses to be extremely heightened. It was an experience I had never had before or since. I was to discover a decade later that it was a walk-in experience by the Ascended Master St. Germain.

In *Puzzle Pieces*, I talked about how we go through a seeking phase. I really stepped up my seeking after that event. I needed to find out even more answers. I was reading books and going to talks. I kept asking from the first level of Knowing with my third-dimensional brain. I shared with you those Aha moments that opened my eyes little by little as I moved through that phase.

As I reflect back, it reminds me of the story where a man finds himself on his roof in a flood. He prays and prays to be saved. A boat comes by and offers to help and the man turns him down. He prays more and more. A helicopter shows up and he turns that away. Finally, the man dies and asks God why he didn't save him. God answers, "I sent a boat and a helicopter."

I had my meditation and journaling practice. Once I had learned how to quiet my mind instead of fighting to get rid of it, I was able to move to a peaceful place and listen. My practice helped a lot. I was able to begin listening and understanding from the second level of Knowing. But third-dimensional life happens and it would rip me out of that space every time. My practice resembled more of an escape.

I was on an emotional rollercoaster of experiences. I would work with the spiritual tools I had learned. Things would be good for a while and I would let things kind of coast. It wouldn't take long to hit an emotional bottom again. After a few of these I learned spirituality isn't a part-time thing or a one-and-done fix. I needed to commit more fully. Questions hounded me. What was I not getting? What was this life about? What is The Game? I found myself again unhappy with my life, a gnawing *feeling* of emptiness that I couldn't seem to fill. I began to demand answers again.

Years passed and I found myself invited to yet another talk on spirituality. I really wasn't interested. I was frustrated with these talks that didn't actually give any real answers I could work with to reach 'that thing' they were always talking about. Inspirational talks, yes, but not much on the how-to. I felt they were leaving something out. It seemed to me they were talking from the place they were at, but not quite giving the critical thing that had gotten them there. Somehow, I was missing a very important key to it all. I felt that once I found that key, everything would be explained. Maybe this time. So, I went. While on the break, I was milling around the tables filled with an abundance of spirituality books that were now available on the market. One book seemed to catch my attention. *Ask and It Is Given* by Esther and Jerry Hicks. It was like it screamed, "Read me!" Remember, books are my thing with Spirit. I bought it.

I began to read *Ask and It Is Given* and during this time there were a lot of things happening in my life. Every time I picked up the book, I felt a vibration of energy that I was not ready for and I had to stop reading. It's as if my life seemed to speed up - things were moving *really fast*. For instance, we were putting our house up for sale and nothing was happening, so we took the house off the market. About this time, I began to read the book for a second time and suddenly even though the house was not on the market anymore people started calling to buy it. I did not understand what was happening. Yet the book kept calling to me. The third time, I made a commitment to myself to read it through to the end no matter what! My life has never been the same. The key was in there and the door for me flew open.

For those who don't know Esther Hicks, she is a trance channel for a group of guides collectively called Abraham. Abraham talked about the Emotional Guidance Scale, the Law of Attraction, and the power of our thoughts in ways I had never heard before. The third level of Knowing was beginning for me. The vibration I felt was my alignment with Spirit and my Soul in a new way. As a result, my life needed to change accordingly, and hence, craziness would follow. I committed to the 22 Processes in Part II of *Ask and It Is Given*.[1] I was prepared to shed the old way of believing about this life experience and step into a new way of Knowing. I picked the red pill so to speak.

Initiations

Initiations are the passing from one awareness level to another on your spiritual journey or leveling up on your Game. Initiations have different emotional *feelings* associated with them depending on the level you are leaving. Some will be ecstasy, while others may *feel* like the grief you *feel* when someone you love suddenly transitions from their physical body. Someone did, the old you. Do not be alarmed. These initial *feelings* are temporary as you adjust to this new level of Knowing.

Right before you slip into a new level of Knowing, you may fear that you are going in the wrong direction or not moving at all. You'll find yourself asking, "What am I doing wrong?" Yep, that *feeling* is your confirmation that something big is about to emerge in your life. You may resonate with this now or not.

Once you have moved into a new level of Knowing, you cannot undo it. You won't lose this level of Knowledge either. Remember my discussion on the Ring Pass Not. The Ring Pass Not is the Law that governs initiations. A student cannot pass to the next level until they have achieved a certain level of Knowledge.

When I speak of Knowledge, I am not referring to mental knowledge. Rather, it is a commitment on the part of the student/ seeker to their Soul/Spirit. It becomes a new lifestyle that incorporates what they have learned and have come to Know in their heart center. This new Knowledge will break down part of the illusion of The Game. You may *feel* like you are unlearning lessons you just discovered on this spiritual journey. Some of the tools you picked up along the way, no longer work. The Game is a little less forgiving of your freewill. You *feel* like *Alice in Wonderland* passing through to the other side of the looking glass. The best part is, you couldn't skip ahead to living Book Three until you lived the first Two.

As you move through this book, I will point out some of the initiations or awareness levels. Some you have already passed through. They happen so quickly sometimes we don't even notice them. We only begin to realize them when we think everyone is on the same page of Knowing and their eyes glaze over because they have no idea what you are talking about. You are trying to share an amazing moment that just happened and they think you have lost your mind. No worries. You are in good company. You may need to find some new peeps to share those stories with.

Meditation and Journaling

The first two books laid the groundwork for this aspect of The Game. I have mentioned meditation and journaling as a daily practice many times and you are going to hear me talk about them even more. I suggest them to anyone I talk with who shares their struggles. Meditation and journaling are the foundation of Spirituality. Do you know that all religions have a form of meditation called prayer?

There is a depth to meditation and journaling. They grow as you grow. There are many types of meditations and journaling, allowing you to choose what fits your moment. Each of your days are different and being fluid with your practice is key to playing The Game. Remember, it took time for me to begin my own practice and it took time for me to fully understand the power meditation and journaling hold. It is a process. It was through my practice that I came to know Spirit, and later, developing a relationship with my Soul. There is no shortcut when choosing to find those answers to the nagging deeper questions you *feel*.

Most of us have heard these words from the French philosopher, Pierre Teilhard de Chardin. "We are not human beings having a spiritual experience. We are spiritual beings having a human experience." Finessing the understanding and the significance of that statement is The Game and it takes a lot of practice to embody this, Knowledge. Your days become a form of meditation traversing the third, fourth, and fifth dimensions. It is not enough to just know the words, but rather to live them. That means discovering for yourself how to live from the inside out.

As we build on our practice, we *feel* lighter. We seem happier. Peace becomes a possibility. Even if you are already in a good place to start with, you will become even happier. There is no limit to how good you can *feel*. Sometimes we just want to *feel* better and we stop there. What if we chose to go beyond *feeling* better and chose to move to amazing? Now I am not suggesting meditating all day. Meditation isn't to escape life. It enhances life. I am suggesting to you that you are able to become an integrated personality.

Oftentimes, meditation is treated as a line item to be checked off the day's to-do list. Meditation, check. What's next on the list today? The mind kicks back into gear and the good-*feeling* alignment created begins to fade rapidly. No, no, no. Your practice is the doorway. Don't close it. Step into it. How do you do that? Begin to move into your day from that same connected *feeling* of Peacefulness, Love, or other good-*feeling* word you choose to describe it as. I don't mean the out-of-body part of your practice, but grounding that good-*feeling* connection you are making into your life experience. The good *feeling*/observer connection. I challenge you to see how long you can go before you are distracted by your mind's need to control everything. Small steps each day. This idea is somewhat controversial because there are many who have a practice who argue that this is not possible. It is possible. It takes practice and commitment. It is what builds the integrated personality.

What is Alignment?

When I speak of alignment with your Soul or with Spirit, as in the Archangels and Ascended Masters and such, I reference moving to a *feeling* place. When you are able to quiet your mind and focus on the present moment, or Now Moment, peace and calm settle in, and maybe a hint of love stirring in your heart center. You may have found those *feelings* weren't connected to anything in particular. That is the vibrational energy of your Soul, Spirit, and All-That-Is. This vibration, we can label as emotions. We may say they *feel* like happiness, Love, Peace. This vibration of God energy is always flowing to you. Always available to you in any moment of your life. It is always your choice to find that alignment and keep it with you throughout your day. It is a very powerful place to be. Remember, your connection to Spirit/your Soul will always *feel* good to you. Unconditional Peace, Love, and Joy.

> Whenever you *feel* Peace, Love, and Joy,
> you are in alignment with your Soul/God/Spirit.
> You are experiencing in that moment the
> true essence of You, your Soul.

Unconditional Peace, Love and Joy

I throw these words around a lot. Make no mistake as I use them it is not by accident or because I read it somewhere. I don't use them lightly. The walk-in experience with St. Germain branded this emotion, vibration, *feeling* into my consciousness in a way that my mind will never argue with. It is a sensation that I cannot easily convey because it doesn't exist in third dimension. As we open our hearts and begin to allow the vibration of our Soul to fill our body, we come to know what that sensation is and only then. Well short of a walk-in from those entities in the ultra-higher realms.

Wait a minute Gwen, I feel love all the time. I love my garden, my pets, my spouse and more. Yes, you do *feel* love. But it is conditional. Your *feeling* of love is contingent on those things or people.

Question. Can you feel that same amount of love for someone who kills or molests children? Or what about politics? Do any of those things get you warm and fuzzy? Probably not because we have a thing called judgment. We love the things we like and are angry with the things we don't, sometimes. Our Souls on the other hand only see the thing with immense love without any judgment, good or bad attached.

I am drilling this in because your Soul holds incredible power as a result of where it resides. Getting to Know and Understand how It *feels* to you is the name of The Game. So, to speak.

Your Now Moment

What is the now moment or present moment? It's not the past or the future, but right here, right now. When you are in the present moment, you are no longer in your mind. The mind has to give way to this awareness moment. As you sit in the now, you can *feel* your physicalness. You begin to *feel* a deeper part of yourself. Inspired thought begins to flow to you and lifts you up. You may cry from the happiness that flows in the moment. This space is where your True Power lies. This moment is your strongest connection to your Soul. How long can you sit in your moment? If you are just starting out, it may take some time to find your now moment. Holding onto that moment becomes the next quest. But our mind can be resistant. It has a lot to say. It will tell you there are things to fear and people to judge.

If at this point, you have not begun your meditation practice, I encourage you to do so. Our goal here is for you to begin to hear what is on your mind. What does your mind think about all day, every day? Those thoughts are what create in your now moment. Any thought you hold onto and give focus to, charged with emotion sets into motion your very powerful ability to create here in the third dimension in ways you will find hard to believe at times. In your very powerful now moment, you are creating in a more intentional way. As you sit quietly and let yourself become the observer and hear the words you think, you begin to see what holds things in place in your life.

> Those thoughts you hold all day are
> your focus of creation.

Unless you take the time to hear those thoughts, you will be caught up in a circle of creations you want to be free of. Besides, when else will you be able to thoroughly and completely hear them without interruption and begin to practice being in your now moment? Too often I hear students say they don't have the time or things are not good right now. Those excuses are the exact reason to sit down and find your alignment. Those excuses are the very thoughts you hold that prevent you from being able to hear Divine Guidance and keeps you from your Glory. Through your practice you begin to take hold of your life and intentionally shift it to the experiences you want. Some experiences that you would have previously thought difficult, you will move through from a place of internal strength and Grace.

Last, your practice holds the energy of commitment. It teaches you the discipline of The Game. You know the door you keep searching for that holds all the answers? Meditation and Journaling are the door. The door to your Soul. Remember the guy in the flood? As much as your mind may want to discount all this, you have nothing to lose by sitting your butt in a chair every day for ten minutes. Just saying.

Focus

Focus. I have used this word often enough, too. It is one you are familiar with. Now we will stop to focus on focus. We will put our full attention on this little word and how powerful it is. The majority of the population doesn't give it a second thought as they wield it around like a sword all day.

As I mentioned, meditation is the practice of focusing your mind. First, we quiet it down, and then we direct it to focus on a given task. Seems sublime enough. Yet, the simple act of getting your mind to agree to sit down and direct it is a big initiation of awareness. It is a dance to last a lifetime. The dance of taking the lead from your mind more and more. Because as you take back control of your life from your mind, you begin to realize where your creating power lies. In your mind's focus. Those thoughts you cling to all day and repeat out loud and to yourself are focused energy you are not usually aware of. Creating all day, every day, non-stop. Where was your mind focused just now?

> Remember: Energy flows where attention goes.

Let me add another layer here. Focus isn't a third-dimensional construct. Spirit creates through focused thought as well. It is how the planet, you, and everything exists. Focused thought. Yes, our physical minds can focus thought, but it does not have the purity of Spirit. Maybe it's time to revisit the topic of the mind.

The Mind

During your meditation and journaling practice, you have been learning to observe your thoughts and how to focus your mind. To control it. To direct it.

Here is a little reminder from Book One on Your Mind.

The mind anchors your Soul to this Game board by being fully immersed or focused in the third dimension. It is an amazing piece of creation. It only exists here in the third dimension and is the perfect tool to make so many things possible. It takes the focus of the mind to create here.

We begin our lives with our minds on autopilot. It is for most intents and purposes allowed to think about whatever it wants to think about whenever it wants to. The mind convinces you to disregard your emotions and anything outside of itself. There are still quite a few people who are unaware of their thoughts. I mean they never give thought to the idea that they have thoughts. They do not have the awareness or the ability to observe their thoughts. That doesn't make them bad people. I am only illustrating one of many, huge awareness initiations you have moved through already.

More and more people with each passing generation do become aware they have thoughts that just keep whirling around in their head all day, every day. Of those, some come to know that they have the ability to change their thoughts and actively set out to do so. Meditation and journaling make us very aware of our thoughts, and it takes a level of skill and practice to listen to those thoughts from a detached place, i.e., observing them. Not letting our mind become fully immersed in the thought threads. This is another big awareness step. The detached observer is the beginning of the integrated personality I will speak on later.

As we observe our mind's thoughts, we soon see it spends a lot of time on the past. Most of us have been fed a diet of fear over the years; those thoughts become very fearful. The mind will regurgitate past failures, losses, and injuries. At the same time, the mind is afraid of the future. It cannot see the future and can paint a fearful picture of what lies ahead based on the past.

A few tips going forward.

- **Any changes in your life experience can scare your mind** and begin a thread of thoughts that ends with, "and then we will die." We usually cut the mind off when it begins this spiral down, and this "stuffing" of emotions leads to a thought process that doesn't stop either consciously or unconsciously. Journaling can quickly let you see those thoughts in their entirety and help you to release them.
- **The mind is happiest** when it has a job to do, like counting during meditation. A fearful mind responds well when reassured that all is well and given examples of wellbeing.
- **GIGO-Garbage in, garbage out.** Whatever the mind has been fed, it will regurgitate. Fear, hate, Love, Peace, or Joy. Going forward, it is important to be mindful of what is on television and who we spend our time with.

Thoughts

"Whether you think you can, or you think you can't--
you're right." Henry Ford

Let's address thoughts. We have them all day long. Thousands of them. Studies say we have upward of 6,000 thoughts per day.[2] Alert! Awareness moment ahead. Maybe you haven't spent a lot of time thinking about or *feeling* your thoughts, but they do carry a charge of energy. Energy that can be labeled as a *good feeling* or not. If at the end of the day most of our thoughts are *good-feeling* thoughts, we move through life *feeling* pretty good, things roll off our backs easily and things are well. Nothing really to do except find more things to love in your day.

However, if we have spent a little too much time focused on *not-so-good feeling* things throughout the day—watching too much nightly news, talking to that friend who loves to spread doom and gloom in the name of being informed, or you have that one thing you just can't let go of—you may be having fewer and fewer *good-feeling* thoughts, and your life will begin to show it. Fear, stress, anxiety, and depression. Thoughts. Thoughts carry powerful vibrational energy.

Once you become aware of your thoughts, things can start to change in your life. I am not talking about changing up the words you use, although that is important, too. I am talking about awareness of how you are *feeling* as you are having those thoughts. Being mindful more often in your day about how you are *feeling* and connecting the thought to the *feeling*. I know it is a little backward, tuning into the *feeling* first and then realizing the thought that is provoking the emotion. This is best achieved by having a strong daily practice. Your practice moves you into a *good-feeling* place at the beginning of your day. Learning to take that *good-feeling* energy with you into your day sets you up for noticing the *not-so-good feeling* when it happens. Yes, this is a big awareness jump here. Noticing when you slip out of your *good-feeling* connection with your Soul/Spirit. Without a *good-feeling* baseline, the *not-so-good feeling* thoughts may be lost in the low simmering boil you have going on.

Why do we want to notice when the *not-so-good feeling* thoughts are upon us? So, we can begin to change our thoughts, the energy, the emotion, the creation. We **can** change our thoughts and thought patterns, even beliefs. I have had many people argue this fact. They say they can't change, and it is true for them because they believe it to be. What follows here will be of no use to those who have shut their mind. Their mind is in complete control. To play at this Game level, you need the ability to be the observer and an understanding of the mind which comes from . . . you guessed it . . . a daily meditation and journaling practice. Your practice allows you to manage The Game.

Our emotions give us a window into where we are with life. Happy or not. Thoughts let us see what we are creating. Good or not. Thoughts of the past are from your Mind. Fearful thoughts of the future are from your Mind. Peaceful thoughts that *feel* good all the time come from your alignment with Spirit, your Soul, and All-That-Is. Let yourself begin to play more with this idea. I think you will be surprised.

Beliefs

What about our beliefs? How does one go about changing those and why?

> "Beliefs are thoughts we keep thinking."
> Abraham-Hicks, *Ask and It Is Given*

I heard this sentence over and over for a number of years. I would nod as if I understood. Then one day the light bulb went on and I shouted, "Beliefs are thoughts we keep thinking." It wasn't until I really embraced my thoughts and actively worked with changing the *feelings* associated with them that I got it. All beliefs are rooted in a thought, a thought that we choose not to let go of. We hold on to it *"believing" it can't be changed.* Believing we can't change something is the very thought that keeps us from our unlimited creative abilities.

If I believe that I can change my thoughts, can I choose to believe I can change my beliefs with new thoughts? It was then I started a new chapter in my life. Which beliefs am I willing to change? It isn't enough to just say the words. It takes living the decision. Get ready. When we make that kind of decision, life will present tons of opportunities to practice it. This concept may be down the road a distance for you right now, but let's plant that seed. We will let it ruminate, and then one day a little sprout will appear and you will wonder if you can really change how you believe. You will find yourself on the other side of the looking glass.

Threads of Consciousness

I want to share this Knowledge about the threads of consciousness, with you. They are your life, Spirit and Soul. There is not a lot of information on this topic and there are variations regarding the locations and names of these threads. For me, this is how I have been taught by Spirit over the years through a bunch of different experiences in this lifetime.

If you are holding this book in your hand and reading these words, your life thread is intact. The life thread is the energy of life that holds this physical body here on planet Earth.

The second thread, Spirit, is connected to the center of the brain, the pineal gland. This is our antenna, if you will, for 'talking' with Spirit. Some points to consider about this thread:

- Most spiritual teachers are tuned into this thread, and depending on their practice, can have a running dialogue with Spirit on many different planes of the universe.

- Mediums tend to tune into the Astral plane, where crossed-over loved ones linger until they move on to their next turn at The Game.

- Some may tune into and refer to Spirit as the overarching God presence, or the Archangels and Ascended Masters and the like, who tend to be anchored in much higher planes of vibration.

- Remember that any information coming through this thread must pass through the physical being's filter of life events and beliefs, hence giving many interpretations of the same message from the Divine. An example: My college days were filled with road trips. Spirit used road trips to express who our guides are.

- This thread passes through the part of the brain where we imagine. Divine Knowledge or Inspiration that comes through may be dismissed by our mind as just imagination.

The third thread, which this book is about, is the Soul thread.

- It is connected to the heart center.
- You may *feel* it as a nudge or Unconditional Love, Peace, and Joy radiating from the heart center.

We will talk more on this thread as we go along.

> All three of these threads are flowing to us, even if we are not aware of them.

The Antahkarana

Building a dialogue with our Soul is called the Antahkarana. Opening that line of communication with Ourselves. Building an awareness of the conversation that is happening every day with your Soul and learning to Trust it and live in unison with it. In other words, creating an integrated personality, an expression of the Soul, or an illuminated personality.

I think this is a perfect place to introduce the Antahkarana, our path or bridge we build to our Soul, and remember, nothing is a straight path with Spirituality. We discover our Truths or puzzle pieces as we come to them based on the life experience our Soul has chosen. We can encounter some truly amazing life experiences and go in directions we never would have thought of for ourselves. This is very true for my life experience to date. What started out as finding happiness turned into discovering Spirit in the form of Archangels and Ascended Masters, to discovering that my Soul had plans and Gwen was along for a ride as a Lightworker.

Lightworkers are Souls whose work is that of guiding others in their Soul's journey and ultimately aiding in the ascension process of the planet and/or universe. Sometimes it *feels* more like a lighthouse in the fog. Guiding them to what exactly? Their Soul. Cracking through the physical mind to allow the Soul to shine through. Lightworkers and Spirit Guides are part of The Game being played on many dimensions.

Most times, our conversations with Spirit are one-sided. We pray, pray, pray. Never really listening. We want something now and we want it a certain way. Expecting those answers outside of ourselves. Very few, venture into building a relationship with their Soul, a relationship that involves a dialogue, or two-way conversation. I think part of that may be because organized religion has frowned on that idea. Can't control the sheep if they are off having their own relationship with God. Ouch! I digress.

One day during meditation, I was receiving information that was amazing. I began to journal; afraid I wouldn't remember it afterward. After my meditation, I felt a nudge to pull out my *Ponder on This* book by Alice Bailey. I was guided to a page where I found the same words I had just written, word for word. In that moment I realized I had just channeled Ascended Master Djwal Khul. This was another one of those moments I had to sit with my mind on. I needed to process what just happened, debating if this had really happened or if it was my ego playing tricks on me. Then I looked at what I had channeled. It was the section on the

Antahkarana. I could *feel* my heart leap in acknowledgment that this was the work we would be doing together. Below is an excerpt on the Antahkarana from the Alice Bailey book *Ponder on This*.

> "8. (2) The Antahkarana is the bridge the man builds—through meditation, understanding and the magical creative work of the soul—between the three aspects of his mind nature. 8. (2) 2. To build or construct a bridge between the brain-mind-soul, thus producing an integrated personality, which is a steady developing expression of the indwelling soul. 8. (2) 3. To build a bridge between the lower mind, soul, and higher mind, so that the illumination of the personality becomes possible."[3]

The Antahkarana: building your bridge or dialogue with your Soul. Let's continue as I show you how it is tied to your emotions, which are linked to your thoughts, which determine your life experience. Let me repeat this point. Your dialogue with your Soul is tied to your emotions, which are linked to your thoughts, which determine your life experience. Soon you will begin to discover for yourself your Soul and what this life is all about for you personally.

Emotions

Our thoughts carry a charge of energy. Energy that can be labeled as having a *good feeling* or not. We have come to label those *feelings* as emotions. Love, Peace, and Joy at the top end of *feeling* good and grief, fear, and depression at the lower end of *feeling* bad with a whole range of other emotions in-between. Throughout my books, you may have noticed how I have mentioned *feelings*. Sometimes asking you directly how you *feel* in the moment. We normally don't pay much attention to our *feelings* unless they are over-the-top, or conversely, hitting rock bottom. We often find ourselves saying we are angry or mad, happy or sad, without truly allowing ourselves to be mindful of the emotion we are talking about and the thought associated with it.

If meditation and journaling are the doors to understanding spirituality, emotions are the key that opens that door. When I first realized this fact, I was caught off guard. All my life, I was never sure where emotions fit into the mix of life in general. I was annoyed by them. I was raised in a family where certain emotions were not allowed, as they were a sign of weakness. Yet rage, anger, and hate flowed freely. It took time for me to understand the role emotions play in The Game. Just as I advocate for a strong meditation and journaling practice, I equally *feel* learning how to work with your emotions properly is essential to The Game and The Antahkarana. I have truly come to know the huge role emotions play in our connection to our Soul and the power it holds.

I get it. People don't want to talk about emotions. Working with our emotions is quickly dismissed by most people. I would see it frequently in my Art of Allowing group over the years when we began to talk about the Emotional Guidance Scale.

"Yeah, yeah Gwen, the Emotional Guidance Scale. I know all about it."

I would ask, "Do you use it?"

I usually heard crickets chirping somewhere.

We would spend a lot of time in the group on the Emotional Guidance Scale and the correct way to work with the emotions we *feel*. Those willing to listen and begin working with their emotions were rewarded with amazing life stories to share.

So, what was the eye opener for me? Why did emotions take center stage in my practice, next to meditation and journaling?

> The distance between you and your Soul can be
> measured by your emotions.

When we are in alignment with who we truly are at our core being, we *feel* that connection as Unconditional Love, Peace, and Joy. The further we move from our Soul's Unconditional Love, Peace, and Joy, the worse we *feel*. We *feel* the distance created by the thoughts we hold in relation to our Soul. The worse we *feel*, the further we are from that alignment. We are *feeling* the rub.

But Gwen, I have over 6,000 thoughts per day. How do I know which are the ones causing the rub? Become sensitive to how you *feel*. What emotions do you *feel*? Yearn to *feel* good more often. Notice when you are not. Learning to use your emotions to find your way back to your alignment with your Soul. I do not wish to villainize emotions that are not pleasant. I do wish for you to begin to embrace them for what they are, an opportunity to stop and shift to a better-feeling thought. Use them to create in a more self-empowered way.

The Law of Attraction is up and running every day, all day. It operates based on vibrations and I just pointed out that we can give these vibrations names. Names like fear, hate, anger, frustration, Love, and Joy. How do you *feel* right now? It will tell you what kind of things you are drawing toward you. Or you can look around at your life. Are there things you don't especially love? If so, that *feeling* associated with the thing has thoughts attached to it, and the vibrations of those thoughts are *not-so-good feelings*. I guarantee it. The longer you hold that not-so-good thought, the longer it will take to move that thing along.

Life happens. We let things and people cause us to not *feel* warm and fuzzy. I get it. I am not immune to stuff. I know there are a lot of books and such out there telling you all about how important it is to be positive and uplifted all the time. Some give you suggestions like affirmations, writing positive statements, or creating vision boards. Always stressing the need to stay positive no matter what because of the Law of Attraction. Unfortunately, this only hints at the vibration, focus, and thought we are holding onto without much awareness. They are addressing the second level of Knowing. These things will help for a little while as you move through the seeking level, but as you learn more, you will *feel* your Soul calling you onto the third level of Knowing. At this point, pretty words won't change anything. It goes deeper than that. You will *feel* the rub even more. Your Soul is calling you.

Let's revisit with this analogy and see if it may help sort out what I mean.

If you were to go to the beach and step into the water until it is up to your neck, that is you at the beginning of your spiritual practice. The water is the slow-moving energy you are in because of your Avatar's vibration. As a result of living your life, your pockets are full of rocks, some big, some small. They don't bother you because the water is supporting you. Then you have an awareness of spirituality. It gets your attention and your vibration begins to speed up. You are moving out of the deep water and toward the beach. The higher the vibration, the more you are coming out of the water, and those rocks are getting heavy and uncomfortable. Time to let go of those rocks.

The rocks represent your old thoughts and belief systems you have been holding onto. The ones that don't *feel* good. Negative thoughts. Working with your meditation and journaling practice as I have suggested, you are able to sort some of the rocks and drop the small ones. But we hold on to some thoughts around big ideas that are not so easily let go of. Some are so old that we don't even know which pocket they are in anymore. How do we find them and begin the process of chipping away at them? Monitoring how you *feel*. If you are happy and smiling, no worries. But in that moment that *feeling* slips away, time to stop and observe what you were just focused on. What was the thought at that moment? Can you hear it? Do you *feel* it? Time for a *better-feeling* thought to hold onto because you are not flowing in the same direction as your Soul.

Working with the Emotional Guidance Scale is an important tool to use at this point. However, it requires more content than I have room for here. Also, changing up some of these thoughts and beliefs is usually a personal journey dealing with a deeper level of Knowing. If you wish to delve deeper into this practice, I am offering online courses to break down the basics, and groups and one-on-one sessions to address your needs more thoroughly. I have found this next level of Knowing is best done with a little support.

The Dialogue Begins

I know I've beat you up about having a practice. I have suggested using it to:

- learn mindfulness in the Now Moment
- hear your ongoing thoughts
- begin to find alignment with Spirit
- take that good *feeling* from your practice into the day
- become mindful when that good *feeling* slips away as you move through your day
- notice the thought in the moment you lose your alignment
- change that thought to a better *feeling* one

Why?
- Thoughts focus the mind.
- Focus creates things.

Thoughts do become things.

Yet there is still a bigger picture going on:

- How you *feel* indicates your alignment with your Soul and Spirit.
- Alignment with your Soul begins your dialogue with your Soul, the Antahkarana.
- The separation of the avatar and the Soul diminishes and becomes an integrated personality, a Oneness. The path of the Ascended Masters.
- An integrated personality begins to master The Game from a different perspective, one through the eyes of the Soul.

Sometimes I refer to this initiation phase as moving to the other side of the looking glass. Many of the earlier lessons and rules you learned in the seeking phase no longer apply. The laws of third dimension can be bent or broken. Your belief system on many topics is called into question. You begin to see The Game. There is an infiniteness to the Unconditional Love, Peace, and Joy of the Soul. The nudges become very important in navigating the landscape of your life. Divine Wisdom flows to you in a wonder-filled way. You discover the Love and Trust you seek is deep within you.

Moving through the pages of these books has been a journey for me and I hope for you as well. You may have a number of stories to share and no one to share them with. Questions keep coming. You keep being called forward, but forward to what? To your Soul. Your Soul has been loving you and you have felt it. It wants you to *feel* that Love and Trust in it. It wants to begin to play The Game with you in earnest now.

Your guides have been along for the ride and showing you the way to that space. Excited to experience with and through you the next level of your journey in this Game. You're developing your dialogue with your Soul. Building the bridge. Now you learn the language of your Soul and discover the real reason your Soul chose this life at this time, was because of you.

Love is the skin of God.

In Love and Gratitude, Namaste

In Love and Gratitude, Namaste, are the parting words of the Angels and Guides before they withdraw their vibration from the Heart Opening Activations. I *feel* complete in what we have shared with you in these books. If I try to add more, it will be ramblings. Yet a part of me knows that we only scratched the surface of what this work holds for you. I hope you take the time to find what resonates with you. Well, I think that is it for now my friends. Blessings.

Work with Gwen

—

I encourage you to visit my website, InsightsandIlluminations. com, which is designed to be more of a community of Avatars exploring their uniqueness and their depth of being. There are classes for all levels of spirituality. Spirit has guided me in creating oracle cards, gratitude beads, journals and more to add a little fun to the whole process. Explore what calls to you. Let's stay connected there or through my blog, newsletter, or social media.

Notes

Book 1: It's a Game

1 Rev. Jack Boland, https://www.truthunity.net/people/jack-boland. It was a radio talk show with Rev. Boland.

2 Mike Mearls and Jeremy Crawford. *Dungeons & Dragons Player's Handbook*, (Renton, WA: Wizards of the Coast, 2014), 4.

3 Matthew Thorpe and Raj Dasgupta, "Benefits of Meditation: 12 Science-Based Benefits of Meditation," Healthline, October 2020, https://www.healthline.com/nutrition/12-benefits-of-meditation. Accessed 21 September 2022.

4 David Masci and Conrad Hackett, "Meditation common across many U.S. religious groups," Pew Research Center, 2 January 2018, https://www.pewresearch.org/fact-tank/2018/01/02/meditation-is-common-across-many-religious-groups-in-the-u-s/. Accessed 21 September 2022.

5 Keely, "Meditation Statistics: How & Why People Meditate in 2022," Mellowed, 14 September 2021, https://mellowed.com/meditation-statistics/. Accessed 21 September 2022.

6 Karen A. Baikie and Kay Wilhelm, "Emotional and Physical Health Benefits of Expressive Writing: Advances in Psychiatric Treatment," Cambridge Core, Cambridge University Press, 2 Jan. 2018, https://doi.org/10.1192/apt.11.5.338.

7 Matthew McConaughey, *Greenlights* (Random House Audio Publishing Group, 2021).

Book 2: Puzzle Pieces

1 Alice Bailey and Djwal Khul, Ponder on This: From the Writings of Alice A. Bailey and the Tibetan Master, Djwal Khul, (New York: Lucis Publishing Company, 2015).

Book 3: Your Soul Connection

1 Esther Hicks and Jerry Hicks, *Ask and It Is Given: Learning to Manifest Your Desires* (Carlsbad, CA: Hay House, 2004), 141–304.

2 Julie Tseng and Jordan Poppenk, "Brain Meta-State Transitions Demarcate Thoughts across Task Contexts Exposing the Mental Noise of Trait Neuroticism," Nature News, Nature Publishing Group, 13 July 2020, https://doi.org/10.1038/s41467-020-17255-9.

3 Alice Bailey and Djwal Khul, Ponder on This: From the Writings of Alice A. Bailey and the Tibetan Master, Djwal Khul, (New York: Lucis Publishing Company, 2015).

About the Author

———

Gwen Peterson wasn't looking to become a spiritual teacher, much less an author. She was looking for a way to feel better. To put joy back into her life. She had the stuff. New home, loving husband, and comfortable lifestyle. It just didn't seem to be enough. There was a nagging feeling. A can't seem to find my happy place feeling. Then like a thunderbolt, her life took a different direction. She found herself having to come to terms with things that didn't fit into her everyday life as she knew it. She found her happy place and so much more. She lives in Naples, Florida soaking up the warmth and beauty it has to offer. Her now ex-husband, Shelby, is her BFF and loves sharing space with her daughter, Misty, and cat, Sebastian. She understands that her journey is still expanding and is content to see where her soul and Spirit lead her. Her days are dedicated to supporting others on their spiritual journey no matter where they are on it. She can be found through her loving online community at InsightsandIlluminations.com.

Made in United States
Orlando, FL
27 December 2022

27796746R00107